Language & Literacy for ELLs

CREATING SYSTEMATIC CHANGE FOR ACADEMIC ACHIEVEMENT

John Seidlitz & Melissa Castillo

EDITED BY
MARGUERITE HARTILL

special thanks
for contributions from

Nancy Motley

Leticia Ruelas

Mónica Lara

Table of Contents

Introduction 6

Chapter 1
Linguistically Accommodating
Instruction for ELLs 11

Chapter 2
Principles of a Language-rich
Interactive Classroom 22

Chapter 3
Creating a Language-rich Inclusive
Environment: Implementing
the First Four Steps 36

Chapter 4
Planning and Delivering Instruction
in a Language-rich Interactive
Classroom 58

Chapter 5
Systematic Implementation 92

Guide to Terms 123

Bibilography 129

Introduction

This book is designed for administrators, specialists, and teachers of English Language Learners (ELLs) committed to improving the educational outcomes of English Language Learners (ELLs).

Consider the following:

- Between 1979 and 2009, the number of school-aged children (5-17 years old) speaking a language other than English, tripled. Those figures represent 4-11 million students, over 20% of all students ages 5-17 (Planty, et al., 2009).
- As compared to English speakers, many ELLs never master English. In addition, they fail to be successful in school at a much higher rate than English speakers (Goldenberg & Coleman, 2010).
- While most ELLs are born in the United States, approximately 80% of ELLs speak Spanish as their first language (Wright, 2010).
- The overwhelming majority of ELLs come from low-income families, and they attend schools serving poor, minority, and ELL students. Usually, these schools have the least experienced teachers and the fewest resources (Wright, 2010).

Additionally, there are legislative and administrative decisions made continually that affect ELL education and those responsible for their education around the country. In states like California, Arizona, and Massachusetts, policies place severe restrictions on bilingual/English as a Second Language or Sheltered Instruction education programs (Wright, 2010). Language policies in Arizona have yet to make a significant impact on decreasing the achievement gap between ELLs and monolingual English speaking students (Garcia, Lawton, & Diniz de Figueiredo, 2010; Gándara et al., 2010) and have failed to benefit ELLs' reading and math attainment (Gándara et al., 2010). The implementation of these language policies has raised concern about equal educational opportunities for language learners in Arizona (Lillie et al., 2010).

The growing numbers of ELLs in K-12 classrooms and the increase of restrictive language policies combined with state and district budgetary concerns can limit the type of instruction and services provided to these students. These factors often leave educators asking, "What can be done to serve ELLs more effectively?" Even in light of the given statistics, we believe that there is much that teachers, administrators, and schools can do to increase the educational achievement of ELLs. It is on this belief that we present this book to you.

The information in this book is based on decades of research combined with findings from a recent study conducted with teachers, coaches, and administrators working with ELLs in the state of Arizona.

In an attempt to respond to policy dilemmas, teacher preparedness, and resources for ELLs in Arizona, the Office of the Vice President for Educational Partnerships at Arizona State University established collaborations with four school districts to create the Institute for Teachers of English Language Learners (ITELL). The institute was a two-year effort focused on targeting academic achievement growth for third and fourth grade ELLs through the implementation of long term, consistent professional development and coaching for teachers of ELLs, after-school learning engagements for ELLs, and opportunities for family engagement. Two schools from each of the participating districts, thirteen teachers, six coaches and four principals participated in ITELL. A mixed methods approach was done in order to determine both quantitatively and qualitatively the impact ITELL had on students, teachers, and instructional coaches.

The professional development and coaching model used in ITELL, "Language and Literacy for ELLs: Creating Systematic Change for Academic Achievement" is presented in this book. *Language and Literacy for ELLs* originated from existing research-based approaches for ELLs, such as the SIOP Model (Echevarria, Vogt, & Short 2012), current research findings (Genesee et al., 2006, Center for Research on Education, Diversity, and Excellence (CREDE); Goldenberg & Coleman, 2010), specifically those of the National Literacy Panel on Language Minority Children and Youth (2006 and 2010), and our personal and professional experiences as ELL educators, researchers, and consultants (Seidlitz & Castillo, 2010). The uniqueness of Language and Literacy for ELLs is its strong emphasis on structured oral language development as a staircase to proficiency in reading and writing.

The content of the model integrates:

- adapted procedures for a language-rich interactive classroom using the Seven Steps approach (Seidlitz & Perryman, 2011).
- methods for implementing and linguistically accommodating curriculum based on English language proficiency levels of students (Seidlitz & Castillo, 2010).
- strategies, coaching, and training for ELL administrators and specialists (Castillo, 2012).

The outcome of the intervention revealed impressive findings. Students instructed by teachers implementing the model improved notably in comparison to students whose teachers did not participate in the ITELL intervention. Specifically, the findings of the ITELL study indicated that while all ELL students improved in reading and math, there was a statistical significance for students at higher levels of proficiency. The gains were measured using the mandated state assessment, i.e., Arizona's Instrument to Measure Standards (AIMS).

	MATH		READING	
AZELLA Levels	Pre-Emergent/ Emergent	Basic Low Intermediate High Intermediate	Pre-Emergent/ Emergent	Basic Low Intermediate High Intermediate
Grade 3	No Statistical Significance	.05	No Statistical Significance	.01
Grade 4	No Statistical Significance	.01	No Statistical Significance	.01

Statistically, what the table demonstrates is that there is statistical significance that the increases shown by basic, low, and high Intermediate ELLs on the state assessment were not random, but can be attributed to the ITELL intervention. There is a 95% chance that increases 3rd grade basic, low/high intermediate ELLs showed in the area of Math can be attributed to the ITELL intervention. There is a 99% chance that increases in reading (for both 3rd/4th grade basic, low/high intermediate ELLs), and the increase in 4th grade Math scores is a result of the intervention (Garcia, et al., 2012).

Qualitative measures demonstrated that as a result of participating in the ITELL professional development and coaching cycles:

- teachers became more aware of how content and language objectives could be better aligned to students' language proficiencies and grade level standards, as well as how academic language can be more effectively modeled for and elicited from students.
- teachers increased the alignment between the classroom activities, student assessments, and content/language objectives included in their lessons.
- there was an increase in the quantity as well as the quality of academic language used both by teachers and by students in ITELL classrooms.
- there was an increase in the type and amount of key vocabulary posted on classroom walls and incorporated into classroom discussions.
- a consistent pattern of strategies was implemented in regard to effective classroom management.

We believe these results were achieved because of the shared emphasis ITELL placed on professional development opportunities and coaching cycles. The professional development opportunities included: identifying the specific needs of ELLs, writing content/language objectives aligned to state content/language standards, structuring language development, linguistically accommodating instruction, and taking additional steps to creating a language-rich interactive classroom. Coaching involved a series of cycles for each teacher and coach; each cycle required a planning conversation (pre-conference), an observation, and a reflecting conversation (post-conference).

Included in this book is an emphasis on providing teachers with the instructional support needed to maximize student potential through professional development and coaching. A brief overview, listed below, provides a summary of each chapter.

A BRIEF OVERVIEW OF CHAPTERS:

Chapter 1: This chapter explains the importance of identifying language proficiency levels and providing appropriate linguistic accommodations.

Chapter 2: This chapter describes the essential principles of a language-rich interactive classroom, or **TIPS**.
- **T**otal participation of all English language learners
- **I**ncorporating academic vocabulary
- **P**romoting academic language and literacy development
- **S**caffolding for all language levels

Chapter 3: Steps 1-4 of the *Seven Steps to a Language-rich Interactive Classroom* are described in this chapter. These steps empower teachers as they develop an inclusive classroom environment, one where ELLs are fully participating members of the learning community. Steps 1-4 are listed below.

   Step 1: Teach students language and strategies to use when they don't know what to do.

   Step 2: Have students speak in complete sentences.

   Step 3: Randomize and rotate with peer rehearsal.

   Step 4: Use total response signals.

Chapter 4: Steps 5-7 of the *Seven Steps to a Language-rich Interactive Classroom* are outlined in this chapter. These steps are the essence of a language-rich interactive classroom; they address the four domains of language, i.e., listening, speaking, reading, and writing, and how they are aligned to language and content objectives.

   Step 5: Set clear content and language goals.

   Step 6: Have students participate in structured conversations.

   Step 7: Have students participate in structured reading and writing tasks.

Chapter 5: This chapter outlines the process for systematic implementation of the seven steps and discusses the ways school districts can systematically change and improve instruction for ELLs.

CHAPTER 1
Linguistically Accommodating Instruction for ELLs

For English Language Learners to be successful in school, their curriculum and instruction must be linguistically accommodated.

Linguistic accommodations are language supports that decrease the language barriers experienced by ELLs as they learn and demonstrate knowledge and skills in English (Texas Education Agency, 2011). Linguistic accommodations give ELLs access to curriculum and opportunities for explicit language development.

A significant part of accommodating for ELLs involves creating a climate of acceptance. All students need to feel comfortable taking the risks that help them develop English proficiency. When ELLs are immersed in a second language without adequate support, there is a sense of overload –also called the affective filter– that can block the ability to learn a new language (Krashen, 1985). The affective filter can be described as an emotional barrier to language acquisition caused by a negative perception to one's environment. Krashen (1985) asserts that, "People acquire second languages only if they obtain comprehensible input and if their affective filters are low enough to allow the input 'in'." Consider the following scenario:

> Mr. Brown is engaged in delivering a lesson to his class that includes 16 native English speakers and 8 ELLs at different levels of language proficiency. His lesson is interrupted abruptly when the secretary brings in a new student, Roberto Martinez. Mr. Brown is frustrated because his class numbers are already high, and he doesn't feel he has the resources he needs to accommodate another student. Roberto is a newcomer who doesn't speak or understand English. The teacher quickly finds a bilingual peer, Leticia, to act as a "buddy" to Roberto so he can continue teaching his lesson, a lecture about the American Revolution. The lesson requires students to listen and take notes. Consider the impression made on Roberto, the new student.

- What is the student feeling?
- What is the affect of this type of introduction on the new student?
- Will the new student be ready to be a risk-taker when learning a new language?
- What could Mr. Brown have done differently?

A welcoming and safe classroom environment must be carefully crafted to create culturally responsive teaching. Culturally Responsive Teaching recognizes that students learn in different ways, and that effective teachers recognize and respond to these differences. This approach focuses on the learning strengths of students, as well as mediates the frequent mismatch between home and school cultures. According to Gay & Howard (2000), teachers of ELLs must "understand how ethnically diverse students learn." This is necessary because the processes of learning – not the intellectual capability to do so – used by students from different ethnic groups are influenced by their cultural socialization. (p. 147). According to Ormond (1995), teachers of linguistically and culturally diverse students must consider ways to:

- measure existing knowledge.
- identify prior success.
- connect new learning to prior knowledge.
- familiarize students with new concepts and information.
- understand how student knowledge is organized and interrelated.

These practices suggest that teachers need to know not only what knowledge and skills students need to acquire but also how students of different backgrounds come to know new information. This will facilitate the organization of their instruction to maximize student learning.

In addition to creating a safe learning environment and a climate of acceptance, teachers of ELLs should possess a functional understanding of Second Language Acquisition theory. Cummins (2003) has been influential to teachers in their understanding of "what it means to know a language and how long it takes ELLs to become proficient in English". He describes two important types of language that we must consider and distinguish between. Those types of language are Basic Interpersonal Communication Skills (BICS) and Cognitive Academic Language Proficiency (CALP).

BICS is described as conversational and informal language used in daily, personal interactions between family members and within social groups. It exists in situational context, it makes communication highly comprehensible, and it tends to be acquired within 1-2 years.

On the other hand, it can take five years or longer for ELLs to develop the type of language called CALP or academic English. Chamot (2009) identifies language functions such as classify, analyze, infer, justify, persuade, solve, synthesize, and evaluate as specific academic language functions. Academic English consists of a variety of linguistic and grammatical structures and language functions that are not typically found in social conversation (Scarcella, 2003). Scarcella illustrates informal versus academic English using the following examples:

- Informal English: *Gimme it* (pointing to a cell phone). *I gotta go.*
- Academic English: *Could you please give me the cell phone because I have to leave?*

The use of informal English is context-rich while academic English is "grammatically correct and is characterized by subordination (because I have to leave) rather than by short, simple sentences. The academic English version does not depend on context to convey meaning" (Scarcella, 2003, p. 66).

In an effort to continue educating students who do not speak English as their first language, programs designed for ELLs "must ensure that students 'keep-up' with age-appropriate academic content while they are learning English" (Valdés, 2001). In the following scenarios, we outline two case studies to illustrate how teachers can give students access to the curriculum while they develop social and academic English skills.

CASE STUDY ONE

Selma, a fourth grader from Mexico, has been in Texas for one year. She is able to access information and respond when the teacher uses visual support and verbal cues. Selma uses basic vocabulary when responding to questions and replies in simple sentences. Selma regularly reads magazines and books in Spanish during her free time. She does not attempt or volunteer to read aloud in English in any content area. Selma, however, has begun to write in English about topics she enjoyed in the Spanish literature she reads.

In response to No Child Left Behind (NCLB), states adopted English Language Proficiency Standards as a way to set targets for ELLS and to measure the degree of English proficiency. The table below is adapted from the English Language Proficiency Standards developed by the states of Arizona and Texas (ELPS). In correspondence with ELPS Texas Proficiency Levels, *figure 1.1* identifies language levels and corresponding language descriptors. Listed at the top of each column are the language domains, i.e., listening, speaking, reading, and writing.

With knowledge of Selma's background, a teacher can use the ELL Proficiency Levels chart to identify her needs in each language proficiency level in each domain. For example:
- Listening – Intermediate
- Speaking – Intermediate
- Reading – Beginning
- Writing –Beginning

Based on the fact that Selma reads a wide variety of magazines and books in Spanish and does not read aloud in English, Selma could be identified at the Beginning level of reading. Selma's teacher could predict that she will read English text slowly, word by word, with a very limited sense of structure.

Figure 1.2 will allow Selma's teacher to specify the type of instruction Selma needs for the remaining domains, i.e., listening, speaking, and writing. Selma will need visuals and prior knowledge in order to comprehend the text. Her teacher will also need to prepare modified or adapted text for Selma to read.

ELL Proficiency Levels *figure 1.1*

Broad Idea Not Exhaustive

LEVEL	LISTENING The student comprehends...	SPEAKING The student speaks...	READING The student reads...	WRITING The student writes...
I *Begin Lit*	• few **simple conversations** with linguistic support • **modified conversation** • few words, **does not seek clarification**, watches others for cues	• using **single words and short phrases** with practiced material; tends to give up on attempts • using limited **bank of key vocabulary** • with **recently practiced familiar material** • with frequent errors that hinder communication • with **pronunciation that inhibits communication**	• little except recently practiced terms, **environmental print**, high frequency words, **concrete words represented by pictures** • slowly, word by word • with very limited sense of English structure • with comprehension of **practiced, familiar text** • with need for **visuals and prior knowledge** • modified and **adapted text**	• with **little ability to use English** • without focus and coherence, conventions, organization, or voice • labels, lists, and copies of printed text and **high-frequency words/phrases** • short and simple, practiced sentences primarily in **present tense with frequent errors** that hinder or prevent understanding
II *Low Beg.* *High Beg*	• unfamiliar language with **linguistic supports** and adaptations • unmodified conversation with **key words** and phrases • with **requests for clarification** by asking speaker to repeat, slow down, or rephrase speech	• with **simple messages** and hesitation to think about meaning • using **basic vocabulary** • with **simple sentence structures** and present tense • with **errors** that inhibit unfamiliar communication • with **pronunciation generally understood** by those familiar with English Language Learners	• wider range of topics and everyday academic language • slowly and rereads • basic language structures • simple sentences with **visual cues, pretaught vocabulary and interaction** • **grade-level texts** with difficulty • at high level with **linguistic accommodation**	• with **limited ability to use English** in content area writing • best on **topics that are highly familiar** with simple English • with **simple oral tone in messages**, high-frequency vocabulary, loosely connected text, repetition of ideas, **mostly in the present tense,** undetailed descriptions, and **frequent errors**
III *Low Int* *High*	• with some processing time, **visuals, verbal cues, and gestures, for unfamiliar conversations** • most unmodified interaction • with occasional **requests** for the speaker to slow down, repeat, rephrase, and **clarify meaning**	• in conversations with some **pauses to restate, repeat, and clarify** • using **content-based and abstract terms** on familiar topics • using **past, present, and future tenses** • using **complex sentences** and grammar with some errors • using **pronunciation usually understood by most**	• abstract grade-level appropriate text • longer **phrases and familiar sentences** appropriately • while developing the ability to construct meaning from text • at **high comprehension level with linguistic support** for unfamiliar topics and to clarify meaning	• grade-level appropriate **ideas with second language support** • with extra need for second language **support when topics are technical and abstract** • with a grasp of basic English usage and some understanding of complex usage with **emerging grade-level appropriate vocabulary** and a more academic tone
IV *Int.* *Adv.*	• longer **discussions on unfamiliar topics** • spoken information nearly **comparable to native speaker** • with few requests for speaker to slow down, repeat, or rephrase	• in **extended discussions** with few pauses • using **abstract content-based vocabulary** except low frequency terms; using idioms • using grammar **nearly comparable to native speaker** • with **few errors** blocking communication • with occasional mispronunciation	• **nearly comparable to native speakers** • **grade appropriate text** correctly • while constructing meaning at near native ability level • with high level of comprehension; with **minimal linguistic support**	• grade-level appropriate **content area ideas with little need for linguistic support** • to develop and demonstrate **grade-level appropriate** writing • nearly **comparable to native speakers** with clarity and precision, with **occasional difficulties** but demonstrates a command of language

Linguistic Accommodation:
Communicating And Scaffolding Instruction *figure 1.2*

Sequence of Language Development	LISTENING Teachers...	SPEAKING Teachers...	READING Teachers...	WRITING Teachers...
I *Entering / Beginning*	• Allow use of same language peer and **native language support** • Expect student to struggle to understand simple conversations • Use **gestures and movement** and other linguistic support to communicate language and expectations	• Provide short **sentence stems** and single words for practice before conversations • **Allow some non-participation** in simple conversations • Provide word bank of key vocabulary • Model **pronunciation of social and academic language**	• Organize reading in **chunks** • Practice **high frequency, concrete terms** • Use **visual and linguistic supports** • Explain classroom **environmental print** • Use adapted text	• Allow **drawing and use of native language** to express concepts • Allow student to use high frequency recently memorized, and **short, simple sentences** • Provide **short, simple sentence stems** with present tense and high frequency vocabulary
II *Low Beg / Emerging / High Beg.*	• Provide **visuals, slower speech, verbal cues,** and **simplified language** • **Pre-teach vocabulary** before discussions and lectures • **Teach phrases** for student to request speakers repeat, slow down, or rephrase speech	• Allow **extra processing time** • Provide **sentence stems** with simple sentence structures and tenses • Model and provide practice in **pronunciation of academic terms**	• Allow wide range of reading • Allow grade-level comprehension and **analysis of tasks** including **drawing** and use of **native language** and peer collaboration • Provide high level of **visual and linguistic supports** with adapted text and **pretaught vocabulary**	• Allow **drawing and use of native language** to express academic concepts • Allow writing on **familiar, concrete topics** • **Avoid assessment of language** errors in content area writing • Provide simple **sentence stems and scaffolded writing assignments**
III *Low Int / Developing*	• Allow some **processing time, visuals, verbal cues, and gestures** for unfamiliar conversations • Provide opportunities for student to request clarification, repetition, and rephrasing	• Allow **extra time** after pauses • Provide **sentence stems** with past, present, future, and complex **grammar,** and vocabulary with **content-based and abstract terms**	• Allow abstract grade-level reading comprehension and analysis with peer support • Provide **visual and linguistic supports** including adapted text for unfamiliar topics	• Provide **grade-level appropriate writing tasks** • Allow abstract and technical writing with linguistic support including teacher **modeling and student interaction** • Provide **complex sentence stems** for scaffolded writing assignments
IV *High Int / Expanding / Bridging / Adv.*	• Allow some **extra time** when academic material is complex and unfamiliar • Provide **visuals, verbal cues, and gestures** when material is complex and unfamiliar	• Provide opportunities for extended **discussions** • Provide **sentence stems** with past, present, future, and **complex grammar** and vocabulary with **content-based and abstract terms**	• Allow abstract grade-level reading • Provide minimal **visual and linguistic supports** • Allow grade level comprehension and **analysis tasks** with **peer collaboration**	• Provide complex **grade-level appropriate writing tasks** • Allow abstract and technical writing with minimal linguistic support • Use **genre analysis** to identify and use features of advanced English writing

LANGUAGE AND LITERACY FOR ENGLISH LANGUAGE LEARNERS

CASE STUDY TWO

Ahmed is a seventh grader who recently arrived in Michigan from Yemen. He is only able to communicate in English using single words and short phrases, and has a limited vocabulary. He reads English text slowly, and often, rereads the text for comprehension. He is able to understand grade level text with some difficulty and he can understand simple sentences with visual cues in a wider range of topics. Ahmed, is able to write in English using high-frequency vocabulary with repetition of ideas.

Even with limited knowledge of Ahmed's background, a teacher can use the ELL Proficiency Levels chart to begin to identify his needs in each language domain, i.e., listening, speaking, reading, and writing.

The State of Michigan, along with 31 others, has adopted English Language Development Standards known as WIDA (World-class Instructional Design Assessment) Standards. The levels include Entering, Emerging, Developing, and Expanding/Bridging. These correspond to Roman Numerals I, II, III, IV on *figure 1.1*. (To view WIDA descriptors, go to http://www.wida.us/standards/CAN_DOs/).

Based on the fact that Ahmed reads a wider range of topics in English but reads slowly and rereads basic language structures, he could be identified at the Developing (II) level in reading. At this point, his teacher can predict that Ahmed will be able to read English text with simple sentences and visual cues. The teacher will also need to prepare modified or adapted text for Ahmed, and will have to pre-teach vocabulary. As indicated by *figure 1.2*, Ahmed's teacher should help him learn speaking skills by providing sentence stems and single words as practice before conversations. In addition, it is important for his teacher to model the pronunciation of social and academic language so Ahmed can participate in structured and unstructured conversations.

Linguistic accommodations ensure that Selma and Ahmed have access to the curriculum and have opportunities to develop social and academic language skills. Other linguistic accommodations can include comprehensible input, differentiation based on language proficiency level, and scaffolding. For example, in *figure 1.2*, under Level I, for Reading, the teacher can see that she will need to organize reading activities into chunks for Selma. By doing this, Selma will have the opportunity to practice high-frequency concrete terms. For Ahmed, the teacher will need to allow him to write about familiar, concrete topics first without assessing the language errors in content-area writing. The teacher will also need to provide simple sentence stems and scaffolded writing assignments for him.

***Differentiating Academic Tasks** by Language Levels (figure 1.3)* provides a list of resources to support groups of students at each language level. Teachers should be strategic in identifying differentiated academic tasks that support groups of ELLs as they participate in the learning process. Under Level I, it is fitting to conclude that ELLs will benefit from the use of illustrations, charts, tables, and graphs representing classroom routines. The use of graphic organizers, pronunciation of social and academic language, and pre-teaching of social and academic vocabulary are also helpful.

On *figure 1.4*, there is a chart that determines ELL language levels within each of the language domains –listening, speaking, reading, and writing. When language data is carefully and thoughtfully examined, ELLs may be found at different levels in each of the language domains. This information can provide educators with insight into areas of strength and need for each student.

Differentiating Academic Tasks by Language Levels *figure 1.3*

I (Entering)	II (Emerging)	III (Developing)	IV (Expanding)
Visuals for classroom vocabulary and academic concepts	Visuals for academic vocabulary and concepts	Visuals for academic vocabulary and concepts	Visuals for academic vocabulary and concepts
Illustrations, charts, tables, and graphs representing classroom routines	Illustrations, chart, tables, and graphs representing classroom routines and some academic concepts	Illustrations, charts, tables and graphs about academic concepts	Charts and graphs about academic concepts
Native language and adapted grade-level texts	Native language and adapted grade-level texts	Adapted grade-level texts	Grade-level texts
Short, simple sentence stems	Simple sentence stems	Variety of sentence stems	Complex sentence stems
Pre-teaching social and academic vocabulary	Pre-teaching social and academic vocabulary	Pre-teaching low frequency, academic and process functional vocabulary	Pre-teaching academic vocabulary and process functional vocabulary
Peer interaction (same language peer, as needed)	Peer Interaction (same language peer, as needed)	Peer interaction	Peer interaction
Native language and adapted writing tasks	Native language and adapted writing tasks	Adapted grade-level writing tasks	Grade-level writing tasks
Gestures for memorization of routines and some academic tasks	Gestures for memorization of academic concepts	Gestures for memorization of academic concepts	
Extensive modeling and guided practice	Modeling & guided practice	Modeling	Modeling
Graphic organizers	Graphic organizers	Graphic organizers	Graphic organizers
Manipulatives	Manipulatives	Manipulatives	Manipulatives
Use of cognates	Use of cognates	Use of cognates	
Pronunciation of social/academic language	Pronunciation of academic terms	Pronunciation of academic terms	Pronunciation of academic terms
Linguistic simplification text*	Linguistic simplification of unfamiliar text*	Linguistic simplification of unfamiliar text*	Variety of grade-level text
Oral translation of words and phrases*	Oral translation of unfamiliar words*	Oral translation of new academic words*	
Bilingual dictionary/glossary*	Bilingual dictionary/glossary*	Bilingual dictionary/glossary*	
Side by side materials*	Side by side materials*	Side by side materials*	

*Guidelines at specific proficiency levels may be beneficial for students at all levels of proficiency depending on the context of instructional delivery, materials, and students' background knowledge.

ELL Language Proficiency Levels *figure 1.4*

Name	Listening	Speaking	Reading	Writing	Composite

CHAPTER 1 Summary

Teachers need to be mindful and to prepare for the ELL learning experience by clearly indentifying and understanding individual student capabilities and cultural backgrounds. With this knowledge, teachers can support and challenge students accordingly. As stated by Seidlitz & Castillo (2010), "Limited language in English does not equate to illiteracy." All students have varied experiences and intelligence, and they need explicit language development to help them learn. The documents and information in this chapter provide teachers of ELLs with resources that should precede the planning process. This material takes the guesswork out of instruction and allows the ELL teacher to anticipate and plan instruction in a purposeful way.

QUESTIONS FOR REFLECTION AND DISCUSSION

1. Why is it important to understand the proficiency levels of your ELLS?
2. What is your current level of awareness of ELL proficiency levels? (class, campus, etc.)
3. What is your current level of awareness of specific linguistic accommodations? (class, campus, etc.)
4. Why is it important to understand linguistic accommodation specific to a proficiency level?

CHAPTER 2
Principles of a Language-rich Interactive Classroom

A language-rich interactive classroom is an environment, which provides opportunities for students to develop social and academic language through oral and written communication.

In a language-rich interactive classroom, teachers clearly focus on two goals: structuring language development and providing opportunities for interaction. Creating and facilitating this type of environment is necessary for ELLs because they benefit from a focus on oracy and multiple opportunities to practice social and academic language.

Oracy is the ability to use language skills and structures necessary for fluent and effective communication. Wilkinson (1970) coined the term to highlight the importance of establishing listening and speaking as essential skills that are "parallel to literacy" (Meiers, 2006). It requires teachers to pay explicit attention to specific language instruction so students can comprehend and express ideas in a variety of contexts. In addition, teachers must focus on providing students with multiple opportunities to practice and apply these learned skills. Dialogue must be included as an essential skill in order to expand the grammatical complexities of speech and vocabulary for ELLs (Escamilla et al., 2010).

To create a language-rich interactive classroom, educators must have a philosophy of instruction that promotes academic language and literacy development through meaningful interaction. In *Language and Literacy for ELLs*, the acronym **TIPS** is used to facilitate the recall of four important principles (adapted from Seidlitz and Perryman, 2011):

- **T**otal participation of all English language learners
- **I**ncorporating academic vocabulary
- **P**romoting academic language and literacy development
- **S**caffolding for all language levels

TOTAL PARTICIPATION FOR ALL ENGLISH LANGUAGE LEARNERS

Total participation requires the inclusion of all students in the classroom, regardless of their language level or ability. Teachers must remember that students learning rigorous content and academic language to meet high academic standards in a second language require specialized instruction to do so. Along with the obvious techniques such as visuals and hands-on, teachers must make a conscious effort to make the learning understandable through a variety of means. It ensures that "every student, during every activity, is involved in listening, writing, speaking, or reading" (Seidlitz and Perryman, 2011, p. 98). Total participation has two essential components that make it successful: comprehensible input and comprehensible output.

Comprehensible input is the ability to understand a message that is slightly above the student's English language proficiency level or as Krashen (1985) describes it, "i + 1 (I plus one). The SIOP Model (Sheltered Instruction Observation Protocol™, (Echevarria, Vogt, & Short, 2008) identifies three features that are critical to maintaining comprehensible input during instruction: using speech appropriate to student proficiency levels, ensuring clear explanations of academic tasks, and employing a variety of techniques to make content comprehensible.

As mentioned in Chapter 1, a significant component of comprehensible input is remembering to create a place where students feel accepted by the teacher and other students, a place where students feel comfortable making mistakes. When the affective filter is high, it is difficult for students to learn a new language. Simple practices such as using a welcoming tone, facing students in class, and pointing to a poster referencing instruction play a significant role in comprehensible input.

Comprehensible output is the effective use of English speech in oral and written communication (Swain, 2005). In order to gradually increase the level of independence, ELLs need daily practice opportunities and repetition of language to negotiate meaning in different contexts. Teachers should begin practicing new language with the whole class by modeling, guiding practice, and giving support before students are able or expected to use it with a partner/s or independently. It is important to pay close attention to the explicit language structure in order to provide students with language practice opportunities. Chapter 4 will outline specific practices teachers can use to elicit oral and written language production from second language learners, such as sentence frames, paragraph frames, and think-alouds.

INCORPORATING ACADEMIC VOCABULARY

Academic vocabulary must be identified, overtly taught, and practiced in order to develop fluency in academic language. Academic language is the language used in textbooks, classroom lectures, and assessments. It includes the, "specialized vocabulary, grammar, discourse/textual, and functional skills associated with academic instruction and mastery of academic material and tasks" (Saunders & Goldenberg, 2010). It tends to be more grammatically complex than social language, and it has more content specific vocabulary. This type of language often poses a formidable task for students, especially ELLs.

Academic language is different from the social language ELL students use outside of classroom situations. For ELLs to be successful in school, they must not only have oral English proficiency, but also, a command of academic English because it enables them to be educationally competitive with native English speakers. Being proficient in informal oral language does not necessarily correlate with success in reading for students. To be successful, they must be proficient in formal oral language. For example, significant research shows that ELLs who perform well on informal oral language proficiency tests — such as the Basic Inventory of Natural Language — do not necessarily perform well on reading assessments. On the other hand, ELLs who perform well on oral proficiency tests with an emphasis on formal academic language — such as the Woodcock language proficiency battery — do tend to perform well on reading assessments (Saunders & Goldenberg, 2010). This shows the vital importance of oral academic language development to teachers of ELLs.

It is important to remember, however, that social language development is still significant for ELLs. Not all ELLs will develop social English before they develop academic English. A student who begins with a high level of proficiency in his/her native academic language may be able to develop an understanding of academic English more rapidly than they can adapt to standard social English conventions. Some ELLs have had the opportunity to study English in its written academic form in their native country prior to coming to the United States. These students may be able to read academic texts in English prior to understanding texts of a social nature, such as notes and e-mails from their English-speaking peers. ELLs may already have a complex schema of academic concepts but may have non-standard or non-English labels for these concepts. If students speak Spanish or another Latin-based language, these labels may be similar, and they may benefit from having teachers make explicit connections between cognates in their primary language and in English. Both social and academic English are necessary for success in a school where instruction is in English. Therefore, teachers of ELLs should create opportunities within content area classes in order to develop both.

Many students classified as ELLs come from lower socio-economic backgrounds. A variety of studies have demonstrated that these students tend to have less academic vocabulary than their middle class and upper class peers (Marzano, 2004). Although many ELLs become proficient in oral language within a few years of attending American schools, this oral proficiency, nonetheless, does not enable them to master grade level content or be successful on standardized assessments. In order to be successful on a standardized assessment, ELLs need to have greater command of the various features of academic language. Command of academic English requires knowledge of a variety of aspects of the language including (Dutro & Kinsella, 2010):

1. phonology (sounds)
2. morphology (affixes, roots)
3. vocabulary
4. syntax (word order)
5. formal and informal discourse
6. social and academic functions

Dutro and Kinsella identify two types of academic vocabulary as brick or mortar words. **Brick** words are the core content area words that are necessary for the mastery of a particular subject. These kinds of words are typically found in the glossary of a content area textbook or in bold or italicized print throughout the textbook. **Mortar** words are the academic words that link brick words together; they make content area text coherent and accessible. Brick words tend to be taught directly and explicitly within content area classes. Mortar words are not typically taught directly in content area classes. Instead, teachers of ELLs must place a greater emphasis on explaining, modeling, and using mortar words in context to ensure success with these words.

Note the chart at the top of the next page with examples of brick and mortar words.

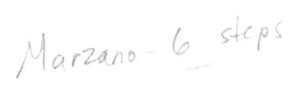

Content Area Examples	MATH Shapes	SCIENCE Water Cycle	LANGUAGE ARTS Literary Elements	SOCIAL STUDIES Revolutionary War
BRICK Content Obligatory Words	polygon, quadrilateral, parallel, rhombus, rectangle, etc.	cumulus, evaporation, precipitation, condensation, etc.	element, character, plot, setting, problem, solution, etc.	Redcoats, revolution, taxations, patriots, representation, etc.
MORTAR Process Functional Words Content Compatible	Compare & Contrast Words: similar different example between therefore	Sequence Words: first next finally	Discussion Words: agree disagree because opinion possibility however	Cause and Effect and Discussion Words: cause effect as a result agree & disagree because opinion possibility however

Marzano (2004) has outlined a six step process for teaching core content terms (brick words) based on his research. They are:

1. The teacher provides a description, explanation, or example of a new term.
2. Students restate the explanation of the new term in their own words.
3. Students create a nonlinguistic representation of the term.
4. Students periodically complete activities that add to their knowledge of terms.
5. Students periodically discuss the terms with one another.
6. Students periodically play vocabulary games with the new terms.

While ELLs benefit from all of Marzano's six steps, an enhanced approach focusing on what research has identified as specific needs is beneficial. ELLs need teachers to focus on pronunciation, spelling, parts of speech, grammar, connotations, and contextual use (Dutro & Kinsella, 2010). The target for explicit instruction must have breadth and depth. Breadth of vocabulary knowledge refers to the understanding and familiarity of a multitude of words, including words used for related concepts. Depth of vocabulary knowledge refers to the understanding and familiarity of various common and uncommon meanings of a given word. Consider the multiple meanings for the word "order."

> **Order** the following numbers from least to greatest.
> The president gave the **order** to send U.S. troops to the Middle East.
> Remember to place your t-shirt **order** by Friday.

Research also indicates that ELLs do better when teachers focus explicitly on word parts (prefixes, suffixes, roots) and when they provide ELLs with opportunities to make explicit links to cognates in their own language (Soltero-González, Escamilla, & Hopewell, 2012). The chart below lists ways teachers can implement Marzano's process in order to accommodate the unique linguistic needs of ELLs.

MARZANO'S STEPS	FOR ELLS	TEACHER/STUDENT
1. Provide a student-friendly description, explanation, or example of the new term.	• pronounce the term, syllable by syllable • have ELLs write the term • use native language to ensure understanding of the new term when possible • explicitly reference or provide opportunity for students to make connections to relevant cognates • identify word parts with cognate connections, if possible • identify parts of speech and how the word is used • provide visual examples and explanations	*This is the word ...* *It is pronounced...* *It is similar to the word ___ (native language term)* *Do you know any words in your language similar to ...?* *The parts of this word are...* *This prefix/root/suffix means ...* *Some examples are ...* *This word is a (noun, verb, adjective, etc.).* *Some examples of this word, in context, are ...*

2. Ask students to restate the description, explanation, or example in their own words.	• model a conversation about a term with a partner
	• allow students to discuss their terms with a partner using native and social language
	• provide sentence stems for beginning ELLs to write descriptions
	• provide written models of word descriptions for students
	• allow students to draw, label, and write descriptions in their native language and to use inter-language strategies, as needed
		Your conversation might sound like this:
		   The term ___ means...
		   It reminds me of ...
		   Your explanation of the term added is...

MARZANO'S STEPS	FOR ELLS	TEACHER/STUDENT

3. Ask students to construct a picture, symbol, or graphic representation of the term.	• provide a model or representation of similar terms
	• provide an opportunity for ELLs to explain their drawing
	• be aware that ELLs may be making valid connections that need to be articulated because of a cultural difference
		Draw a picture representing...
		Explain to a neighbor why you represented ___ that way.
		You might use phrases such as
		   I drew a....
		   To me it means ___ because ...

4. Periodically, engage students in structured vocabulary discussions that help them add to their knowledge of vocabulary items.	• encourage students to connect terms to their own experiences inside and outside of school
	• provide stems and model conversations during discussions
		Tell your partner why the term ___ is familiar to you. You can use the stem:
		   _____ reminds me of...
		   I've seen the term _____ in/at ....

5. Periodically, ask students to discuss the terms.	• have ELLs interact with L1 and L2 dominant peers during interactions where terms are discussed
	• provide stems for comparing, contrasting, and constructing analogies
		See how the other members of your group explained the term ....
		Talk to your partner about the term _____ using the stems...
		   _____ is similar to/different from _____ because ....
		   _____ is to _____ as _____ is to ...

6. Periodically, involve students in games that allow them to play with the terms.	• make sure ELLs of all proficiency levels are fully included in the games
	• provide models and language stems, as necessary
	• explain any hidden cultural expectations of games (volume, tone, competitive language, etc.)
		We're going to play ...
		During the game, you can use the phrases ...
		   It should look like ....
		   It should sound like ....

One of the most important things educators can do to improve vocabulary instruction is to think critically about current practices. The following chart provides opportunities for teachers to reflect on vocabulary selection methods for ELLs.

SELECTING WORDS FOR DIRECT INSTRUCTION

- How does the word support mastery of the objective?
- Will students encounter this word across multiple content areas? (e.g., define, justify, identify)
- How frequently does the word appear within the text?
- Is this a word that students will require for comprehension of the text?
- Is this an unknown word that can be taught in passing with a visual or a gesture? (e.g., nautical, vessel, forlorn, fumble)
- Can students determine the meaning of the word by its prefix or suffix?
- Is this a word that students should anchor in long-term memory?

PROMOTING ACADEMIC LANGUAGE AND LITERACY

For ELLs to excel in school, educators must focus on both language and literacy development. Although literacy and language are related concepts, they have clear distinctions. Understanding the differences between a focus on literacy, as opposed to a focus on language, will help ELL educators plan and deliver effective lessons to address both concepts.

Literacy is defined in a variety of ways, and the concept of literacy has evolved significantly. Webster's Dictionary provides two definitions of literacy that are somewhat reflective of current thought. One definition of literacy describes it as the ability to read and write. This is the definition most educators recall when they hear the term literacy. For example, if we hear that a nation has a low literacy rate, we understand that a large number of citizens lack the ability to read and write in the language of that country. Webster's Dictionary also defines literacy as knowledge of a particular subject area. For example, the National Center for Science Education (NCSE, 2013), describes scientific literacy as, "the knowledge and understanding of scientific concepts and processes required for personal decision-making, participation in civic/cultural affairs, and economic productivity."

To understand this definition of literacy, it is helpful to reflect on the question, "What exactly does it mean to be a literate person?" Becoming a literate person involves more than the skill of decoding text and comprehending meaning. Achieving literacy involves developing a broad schema that includes specific knowledge of a variety of subjects, enabling one to communicate in a particular environment. A large part of becoming literate in a school environment means being able to navigate academic content in a particular discipline.

Because language is "the primary vehicle for intellectual development," (Echevarria, Vogt, & Short, 2008) literacy and language development are significantly related to one another. The primary focus of literacy development is fostering academically literate students who can navigate a variety of academic subjects, and the goal of language development is to develop fluency in social and academic English.

To better understand language development, it is helpful to reflect on yet another question, "What does it mean to be fluent in a particular language?" Fluency involves more than being able to speak a language. To be fluent in academic English, one must be able to read, write, listen, and speak in a variety of contexts with a variety of goals. A fluent speaker needs a deep understanding of the phonology, morphology, syntax, vocabulary, and pragmatics of words and language.

Content objectives   *Language Objectives*

In order to facilitate literacy and language development, teachers of ELLs must focus on both in every lesson. This especially holds true for teachers in ESL/ELD (English as a Second Language or English Language Development) classes and sheltered/content area classes. Research on ELL instruction indicates that an approach focusing on two separate objectives —a content objective and a language objective —is an effective way to meet these two goals for ELLs (Echevarria, Vogt, & Short, 2008; Goldenberg & Coleman, 2010; Castillo, 2012).

Content objectives focus on developing a deep understanding of the content and schema that promote literacy. Content objectives are aligned to the state standards of any given state and to a particular level of Bloom's taxonomy. Language objectives focus on developing targeted language forms and functions in English (Norris & Ortega, 2000). Language objectives can be aligned to the language proficiency standards of each state and a specific language process for reading, writing, listening and speaking. The distinction between content and language objectives and how to write them effectively will be addressed in more depth in Chapter 4. The following table addresses the similarities and differences between the two:

CONTENT OBJECTIVES	BOTH	LANGUAGE OBJECTIVES
• align with grade-level standards	• have clearly planned and written goals for daily lessons	• are aligned with English Language Proficiency Standards and reinforce and provide access to grade-level standards
• build knowledge of topics tied to grade-level standards	• identify what students should know and be able to do	• build students' ability to listen, speak, read, and write about grade level topics tied to grade-level standards
• are goals that incorporate techniques to explicitly support and develop content understanding	• guide teaching and learning	• have goals that incorporate techniques to explicitly support and develop academic language
• provide the context for the development of academic language	• are measurable and observable	
	• express a complete idea and can be assessed	
• are appropriate to students' level of knowledge about content	• ==are written and stated in appropriate student friendly grade-level academic language==	• provide processes for Second Language Acquisition
		• are appropriate to students' language proficiency
• meet district and state goals for content mastery (AYP, NCLB, etc.)	• are differentiated based upon knowledge and language proficiency levels of all students	• can bring focus to the pragmatic purposes of language (functional language such as transitional words, descriptive words, etc.)
	• allow for students to demonstrate higher-order thinking skills	• meet district and state goals for English language proficiency (AYP, NCLB, etc.)

SCAFFOLDING FOR ALL LANGUAGE LEVELS

It is essential for teachers of ELLs to scaffold instruction. In doing so, they provide student support that leads to independence. In the context of language development, scaffolding provides specific targeted support so that students gradually become self-sufficient in their language production. The SIOP model identifies three ways teachers can scaffold instruction for ELLs (Echevarria, Vogt, & Short, 2008):

- oral scaffolding
- procedural scaffolding
- instructional scaffolding

Oral scaffolding is the use of oral language that includes teacher modeling and support. Examples of oral scaffolding include recasting (repeating a student's response with correct English structures), rephrasing student responses, paraphrasing, and providing appropriate wait time. When providing oral scaffolding to students, it is unnecessary to have students repeat responses once they are recasted, paraphrased, or rephrased. Note the examples below:

Teacher:	What is the first step in the life cycle of a frog? Selma?
Selma:	Um...to...
Teacher:	The first step in the life cycle is...
Selma:	The first step in the life cycle is that the frog lays eggs.
Teacher:	Yes. The first step is that the frog lays eggs. Selma, say, "The first step in the life cycle is that the frog lays eggs."
Selma:	The first step is...
Teacher:	The first step in the life cycle of a frog is...
Selma:	The first step in the...
Teacher:	The first step in the life cycle of a frog is...
Selma:	The first step in the life cycle of a frog is...
Teacher:	The frog lays eggs.
Selma:	The frog lays eggs.
Teacher:	Now say the whole sentence again.

Oral Scaffolding – Wait time
  rephrasing
  paraphrasing
  recasting

Selma is probably feeling defeated by the end of this exchange. By forcing her to repeat the sentence over and over, the teacher creates undue stress and lowers student enthusiasm and willingness to answer subsequent questions. The intent of the communication is lost with such frequent repetition, and in fact, the interaction isolates Selma from the rest of the class. Students who hear this dialogue in class will most likely become distracted, disengaged, and probably very bored. Compare it to the example below:

Oral scaffolding

Teacher:	Take some private think time to formulate an answer to this question: What are some of the effects of global warming?
Teacher:	When you have an answer, put your hand on your shoulder. *Wait time*
Teacher:	You can share your thoughts with a partner using this sentence stem: Some of the effects of global warming are... Class, please read the sentence with me. (Students then share.)
Teacher:	(The teacher calls on Selma after she's had a chance to practice with a partner.)
Selma:	Some... um...of ...
Teacher:	Some of the effects of global warming are...
Selma:	Some of the effects of global warming are that the water is going up.
Teacher:	Correct. The sea level is rising. *rephrasing*

Given a sentence stem, Selma now has the language she needs to articulate a response. She is also given the opportunity to practice her response with a partner before she is called on to share with her classmates. Since she is reminded of the stem in a non-threatening way, she ultimately shares.

Procedural scaffolding gradually increases the level of ELL independence (Fisher & Frey, 2007). Teachers provide procedural scaffolding through three sequential processes: I do, We do, You do. See figure at right. In the **I do** process of the lesson, the teacher explicitly introduces, teaches, and models the content and academic language students are expected to develop. In the **We do** process, teachers provide students with guided practice for the new content and language. Teachers measure student comprehension and make appropriate modifications or provide additional supports as needed. Opportunities exist, in this step, for students to work with peers in small groups or in pairs. Finally, the **You do** process facilitates independent student application of the content and language objectives, allowing teachers to measure student understanding and learning.

Instructional scaffolding is the third type of scaffolding and includes support for language output. Instructional scaffolding facilitates independent use and access to the English language by explicitly teaching linguistic structures and strategies. Examples of instructional scaffolding include paragraph frames, think-alouds, and graphic organizers which provide processes to organize thinking in order to produce language.

CHAPTER 2 Summary

TIPS principles help teachers understand how to engage students in the learning process, as well as how to provide necessary student support.

>   **T**otal participation for all ELLs
>   **I**ncorporating academic vocabulary
>   **P**romoting academic language and literacy
>   **S**caffolding for all language levels

TIPS ensures that ELLs are the central focus of instruction and learning. By including all of the elements of TIPS, there is a guarantee of adequate inclusion and support for ELLs which offers an equitable opportunity for them to obtain academic success.

QUESTIONS FOR REFLECTION AND DISCUSSION

1. Why is it important for educators to understand TIPS—the principles behind a language-rich interactive classroom?

2. What current practices are in place at your school/district that align with TIPS?

3. How could the principles be shared and/or discussed in order to build awareness at your school/district?

4. What might be challenging for educators of ELLs at your school/district?

CHAPTER 3
Creating a Language-rich Inclusive Environment
Implementing the First Four Steps

Implementing the first four steps of a language-rich interactive classroom establishes a platform for ELLs to participate in the learning process in meaningful ways.

It gives students the environment and structure to develop academic content and English language proficiency. The first four steps will have an immediate effect on the quantity and quality of active responses students contribute in any given lesson.

STEP ONE

Teach students strategies and language to use when they don't know what to do.

Language learning strategies can be defined as those specific behaviors and skills that improve a student's ability to listen, speak, read, and write in English. Examples of language learning strategies include:

- clarification
- explicit vocabulary development
- repeated rehearsal
- working with peers

In order to better understand learning strategies and their effect on ELLs, we have categorized them into four strands: social/affective, meta-cognitive, cognitive, and language learning strategies.

Social/affective learning strategies are the various ways students interact with others and the way they use emotional resources to increase learning abilities (O'Malley & Chamot, 1990). If ELLs do not feel accepted and valued, it will inhibit their ability to learn strategies and content in class. ELLs do not learn academic concepts and language skills in a vacuum, but rather in the company of others. One critical difficulty ELLs face is socializing successfully with their peers (Rolstad, Mahoney, & Glass, 2005). With that understanding, social/affective learning strategies must be addressed first. ELLs need to feel accepted by their peer group, who often consider them outsiders. Conversing socially helps break down barriers for ELLs (Rolstad, Mahoney, & Glass, 2005). Then, and only then, can they comfortably contribute to a social or school group. As stated in Chapter 1, we must reinforce the notion that teachers have to consider the social language development of the ELL. In fact, when ELLs are taught how to overcome inhibitions, how to participate in a group, and how to navigate the complex social dynamics of a diverse classroom, they are equipped with strategies that let them engage in the classroom community and subject content.

[handwritten: thinking about our thinking]

Meta-cognitive learning strategies are ways that students spend time reflecting on their own thinking and learning (Short & Fitzsimmons, 2007). When students begin to think about their own learning, they start to notice how they learn, how others learn, and how they might adjust in order to learn more efficiently. Self-questioning is an example of a meta-cognitive strategy that helps ELLs become more successful (Echevarria, Vogt, & Short, 2008). For example, during metacognitive thinking, students can look at a math problem and ask themselves, "What steps did I use to solve this problem last time?" This question allows them to be better equipped to solve problems in the future. Similarly, students who ask themselves, "Did that make sense?" after reading a paragraph from a textbook dramatically increase comprehension of new material.

[handwritten: Tools we use to reinforce or close gaps in learning]

Cognitive learning strategies are tools or processes that enable students to complete complex tasks. When students embrace a strategy to help them think through and complete a task, they activate a cognitive learning strategy. Activating prior knowledge before beginning a science experiment, using a graphic organizer to plan an essay, and summarizing information from a reading passage are all examples of cognitive strategies that help ELLs successfully complete academic tasks. Because the majority of academic tasks facing ELLs are complex and rigorously layered, using cognitive learning strategies is crucial to their academic success.

The following table outlines examples that make the instruction of learning strategies more concrete for teachers and ELLs. This is not an exhaustive list but rather a sampling to identify examples within each strand.

LANGUAGE	SOCIAL/AFFECTIVE	META-COGNITIVE	COGNITIVE
Sentence Stems	Cooperative Groups	Access Information Sources	Use Newly Learned Information
Repeat and Rephrase	Structured Interaction	Reflect on New Information	Activate Prior Knowledge
Paraphrase	Partner Sharing		Summarize
Visualize	Group Discussion	Make Connections	Highlight Key Information
Explicit Vocabulary Instruction	Ask Questions	Monitor and Clarify	Reread
	Encourage Yourself		Use Graphic Organizers
	Self-Talk		Make a Plan
			Identify How Information is Organized

Before teachers begin to teach learning strategies explicitly, they should consider the learning strategies students are already demonstrating. Then, students can be encouraged to try new strategies instead of relying on strategies that may not be working. While it is helpful to teach specific learning strategies one at a time, the process is not linear. Teachers can use more than one strategy at a time, moving and incorporating others when new information is introduced.

In addition to teaching ELLs specific learning strategies like the ones discussed in this chapter, students must also have specific language to use when they do not know what to say or do. Displaying clarifying questions or content specific sentence stems on the walls of the classroom or in student journals are effective ways to ensure that students have access to the language they need to use when communicating. The examples that follow provide students with the language they need to form a response.

Sentence Stems to Use for Teaching Learning Strategies

LANGUAGE	SOCIAL/AFFECTIVE	META-COGNITIVE	COGNITIVE
Can you help me…?	I can find information by…	I can use the word ____ when…	You said ____. I think that means…
I think/believe…	This reminds me of…	____ means…	Can you please repeat that?
I do not understand…	Let me say that again…	I can explain…	I can visualize…
I can do …	How would I be able to check…	I know…	I think you are asking… and ____ means…
When I get confused, I can…	I mean…	I want to know…	I can use the word ____ to…
Our ideas are the same because…	This is like…	It's about…	I can use ____ to organize…
Our ideas are different because…		I can reread to find…	When I have to ____ I need to…
I heard you say…		My plan is…	
		The key words are…	
		This is organized by….	
		The general idea is…	

Teachers might ask, *"How might I implement Step One? How do I teach students strategies and language to use when they do not know what to say or do?"*

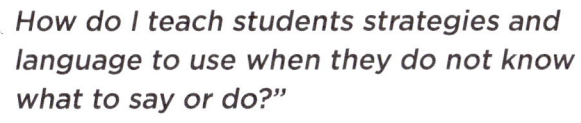

In order for ELLs to try out a new strategy or speak a new language, teachers can and should address the social/affective needs of students. When students do not know what to do or say, for example, options need to be available to them. One option can be seen on the poster to the right.

Essentially, this poster lists alternatives to saying, "I don't know." If a poster is not available, teachers can create a similar resource using chart paper. ELLs however, will not be able to use these questions until they are given explicit instruction explaining: what the questions are asking, how to use each question,

INSTEAD OF I DON'T KNOW…

*MAY I PLEASE have some more information?

MAY I HAVE some time to think?

*WOULD YOU PLEASE repeat the question?

WHERE COULD I find more information about that?

*MAY I ASK A FRIEND for help?

Seidlitz EDUCATION

CHAPTER 3: Creating a Language-rich Inclusive Environment   39

and when it is appropriate to ask each question. This type of explicit instruction addresses three types of knowledge from which ELLs benefit:
- declarative (What is the strategy?)
- procedural (How do I use the strategy?)
- conditional (When and why do I use the strategy?)

According to experts, learning strategy instruction that includes declarative, procedural, and conditional knowledge increases an ELL's ability to use learning strategies effectively (Echevarria, Vogt, & Short, 2008; Lipson & Wixson, 2003). Conversation with students about the questions on the poster (or any other learning strategy) should include:
- an explanation of what the question means (what the strategy is)
- the appropriate time to ask that type of question (the strategy used in the appropriate context)
- the type of answer a student can anticipate when asking that question (when and why will the the strategy help me)

The box below provides an example of how to address the first question on the poster, "May I please have some more information?"

> Today we are going to talk about what you can do if I call on you to answer a question and you don't know the answer. Everyone look up here at this poster (pointing to the poster). The title says, "Instead of I don't know," (underlining the title with your finger) and then there are five questions listed below. The reason we have five questions is because there are many different reasons you might not know an answer. Each one of these questions (pointing to the questions) will give you a different kind of help. If you are unsure of what to say, you can think about what kind of help you need and then select a question from the poster.
>
> Today we're going to look at the first question, "May I please have more information?" Repeat after me, "May I please have more information?" This means, "Can you tell me or show me something else to help me answer the question?" When you ask me that, I will give you a different example, some new words, or another clue to help you with your answer. Please turn to a neighbor and clarify for him/her the meaning of, "May I please have more information?". If you need some help from me, please raise your hand.

When students use the questions on the poster to help them respond, they are actively engaging in the learning process. We want students to ask themselves:

"Which one of the questions will help get me to an appropriate response?"

"What do I need right now in order to support my understanding and to participate in class?"

When using the "Instead of I don't know" poster, be sure to call on the student who originally responded, in order to assess his/her application of the newly-learned strategy. This might seem obvious in the beginning, but there can be challenges. For example, it is easy to forget the student who originally responded if he/she asks for some time to think. Or, when a student asks a friend for help, it is appealing to accept the friend's response in order to move on more quickly. When teachers fail to return to the original student, the student is denied the chance to use a learning strategy, and has not been held accountable for responding.

As the phrase "I don't know" is eliminated from the classroom, students can use other learning strategies to become more sophisticated when thinking about their own learning processes. There are also ways to help students become more skilled at selecting strategies that help them complete various academic tasks in the best possible way.

Keep in mind the following ideas as you begin to implement Step One:
- Give students the appropriate amount of information they need to answer questions on their own.
- Build in whole class wait time before asking a question.
- Allow students to share with a partner before sharing with the whole class.
- Name the strategy students use and acknowledge them for using it.
- Use the think-aloud process when employing learning strategies.

Step 1: Teach students language and strategies to use when they don't know what to do

STEP 1 Summary

When students are held accountable for responding and when they are explicitly taught language and learning strategies to help them respond, they become empowered to take charge of their learning. Step One, using meta-cognitive strategies (Duffy, 2003), teaches ELLs to monitor their own thinking, determine whether or not they understand, choose a way to access help, and explore different learning strategies (Chamot, 2009). This step also builds self-efficacy for ELLs, and the strategies and language they acquire will be useful inside and outside the classroom.

→ that's the goal, to transfer

STEP TWO

Have students speak in complete sentences.

In Step Two, the development of high levels of English oral language proficiency is the priority. Academic success in the United States requires proficiency in oral English (Goldmanenburg & Coleman, 2010). Consequently, students must go beyond knowing vocabulary words; they must learn how to form and structure these words in the academic language they read, write, and speak. They need to know how to express complex meanings orally even if they are limited in English language proficiency. Teachers must remember that students have trouble writing in ways they cannot speak. The expectation and preparation of students to respond in complete sentences allows them to participate in learning in a formal way. Although it must be appropriate for their language level, ELLs will perform better if there are set expectations based on academic achievement rather than solely on language proficiency levels. Second language research suggests the need to pay attention to both second language acquisition and language form (Schmidt, 2010). Having students share and respond to both the teacher and other students using complete sentences with specific grammatical structures can be a successful integrated approach to teaching ELLs the forms and meanings of English. Similarly, it facilitates the opportunity to assess both language and literacy development.

Having students speak in complete sentences provides a process for students to hear content area vocabulary used in context, not only by the teacher, but also by their peers. The National Literacy Panel on Language Minority Children and Youth (2008) highlighted the significant relationship between oral proficiency in English and reading and writing proficiency. When students are proficient in oral language, they are more proficient in their reading and writing (Jean & Geva, 2009). The SIOP model (Echevarria, Vogt, & Short, 2008) advocates the idea that students need frequent opportunities for interaction in order to encourage elaborated responses about lesson concepts. A classroom culture that requires the use of complete sentences routinely fosters student elaboration while a classroom using one-word responses to questions does not. Students need to use content language accurately when they speak, and they must hear the language multiple times and in multiple contexts.

Additionally, speaking in complete sentences exposes ELLs to examples and practice of both the form and the function of various messages. Form and function will be discussed further in the next chapter. A significant part of mastering academic English means possessing semantic and syntactic knowledge in addition to using functional language (Echevarria, Vogt, & Short, 2008). In other words, students must understand advanced language structures in order to master the language used in school. The two examples below illustrate this point:

- When the eggs hatch, most birds feed their young until they are strong enough to find their own food (Smith & Ragan, 2005).
- A conclusion was reached that pH determined the rate.

The language is basic; however, the structure is complex. In both samples, students may lack comprehension even though they know the meaning of all the words. When ELLs are taught how to put words together to express meaning (form), understand the various reasons for communication (function), and navigate oral and written communication, their English language proficiency increases. ELLs need to know that language is used for many different reasons, and the way words are put together (form) depends upon our reason (function) for using the language. Students use language for many functions: to explain, to summarize, to ask, to defend, to connect, to clarify, to compare, etc. A teacher's job is to explicitly show how to articulate those functions by giving students access to many different forms of language. Below are two sample interactions to illustrate the power of this technique:

EIGHTH GRADE CLASSROOM A	EIGHTH GRADE CLASSROOM B
Teacher: Okay class, yesterday we discussed the three branches of government. Let's see if we can remember what those are. Sonia, can you tell us the three branches of government?	Teacher: Okay class, yesterday we discussed the three branches of government. Let's see if we can remember what those are. Sonia, can you tell us the three branches of government?
Sonia: Executive, Legislative, and the one with the judges.	Sonia: The three branches of government are the executive branch, the legislative branch, and the one with the judges.
Teacher: Judicial, that's right. What is the judicial branch responsible for doing?	Teacher: The judicial branch, that's right. What is the judicial branch responsible for doing?
Sonia: The court cases.	Sonia: I think the judicial branch is responsible for, um, mostly listening to cases in court and deciding who is right and wrong.
Teacher: Good. Everyone take out your homework and find question 3, which asks about the judicial branch. Joey, what did you select?	Teacher: Good. Everyone take out your homework and find question 3, which asks about the judicial branch. Joey, what did you select?
Joey: Umm, for #3? Uh, C.	Joey: Umm for #3? Uh... the responsibilities of the judicial branch include: C. interpreting the Constitution and deciding cases.
Teacher: That's right. The responsibilities of the judicial branch include: C. interpreting the Constitution and deciding cases.	Teacher: That's right.

FIFTH GRADE CLASSROOM A	FIFTH GRADE CLASSROOM B
Teacher: Okay class, yesterday we talked about all the different parts of a story. We called them literary elements. Sonia, can you remember one of the literary elements we talked about?	Teacher: Okay class, yesterday we talked about all the different parts of a story. We called them literary elements. Sonia, can you remember one of the literary elements we talked about?
Sonia: Problem.	Sonia: One of the literary elements is the problem.
Teacher: The problem. That is one of the literary elements. What is the problem in a story?	Teacher: The problem is one of the literary elements. What is the problem in a story?
Sonia: The bad part.	Sonia: It is the bad part in the story.
Teacher: Tell me more.	Teacher: Tell me more.
Sonia: Like fixing the wrong part.	Sonia: It's like fixing the wrong part. The problem has to get fixed.
Teacher: Okay. Good. Joey, what is another literary element we discussed yesterday?	Teacher: Okay. Good. Joey, what is another literary element we discussed yesterday?
Joey: Umm...	Joey: Umm...
Teacher: What is another important part of every story?	Teacher: What is another important part of every story?
Joey: People, umm, the characters.	Joey: Another important part is the people, umm, the characters.
	Teacher: That's right.

In classroom A, there is no expectation for students to use complete sentences; whereas, in classroom B there is. It is clear in both conversations that Sonia and Joey have some content understanding. However, it is only in Sample B that their communication reflects their social studies and language arts class content.

Step Two is beneficial to students because it gives them practice with academic language. In the example at the beginning of Step Two, Sonia and Joey had the correct answer in both samples, but only in sample B did they speak using the words of the content area –executive, legislative, and judicial. They also used other academic terms such as responsibilities and include. **Speaking in complete sentences about content concepts** increases exposure to both the social and academic language necessary to communicate content. With each exposure, students advance communication skills and deepen understanding of the content.

When complete sentences are used in the classroom, students are continually exposed to the formal language structures of school and the professional world. ELLs benefit from practicing complex sentence syntax because it broadens the scope of their oral language proficiency. Learning English is not just about knowing how to say words in English, but also about how to combine those words in a structure that clearly communicates a message in a contextually appropriate manner. Speaking in complete sentences prepares ELLs to be successful communicators in the classroom, in a career, and in life.

As Step Two is implemented, remember:

- Students do not need to speak in complete sentences all the time.
- We must explicitly teach ELLs about the form and function of language.
- Sentence stems provide the necessary language support ELLs need in order to speak in complete sentences.
- The form and function of the sentence stem should match the level of cognition in the lesson objectives.

How do I implement Step Two? How do I have students speak using complete sentences?

In this step, teachers of ELLs are responsible for modeling, guiding, and helping students practice using complete sentences. For example, when students ask if they can work with a partner, teachers can respond by saying, "Yes, you may work with a partner," instead of, "Sure." Or, when a student asks, "What do I highlight?" teachers can respond by saying, "Please highlight all the persuasive language," instead of, "The persuasive language."

Another critical aspect of implementing Step Two is to explicitly show students how to create a complete sentence. This can be accomplished by teaching contextualized grammar lessons associated with complete thoughts. Students can be taught how to use the language of the question to begin an answer. For example, if teachers ask, "What is the conflict in the story?" students can respond by saying, "The conflict in the story is…" Recasting or restating is another effective and instructive way to model formal language structures. When a student offers a phrase or a one-word response, teachers can recast, or restate, the content of their response in a complete sentence. For example:

> Teacher: Which one of Newton's laws of motion did our experiment illustrate?
> Marco: His first.
> Teacher: Our experiment illustrated Newton's first law of motion. That's right.

Even with consistent modeling, ELLs often need additional support in order to speak in complete sentences. They may know what they want to say, but they may be unsure about how to say it. Providing sentence stems, or sentence starters, can help students overcome this difficulty. A sentence stem is a short phrase that provides a structure for students as they begin to speak in complete sentences.

A general stem is a sentence starter that is cross-curricular. Specific stems apply to a particular lesson context. By providing both general and content specific sentence stems, students increase their communication skills as they process and master academic content. Some examples include:

GENERAL STEMS	CONTENT SPECIFIC STEMS
I believe…	This shape is…
In my opinion…	I would support Sam Houston because…
First,… next,… and finally,…	One characteristic of the rain forest is…
One reason could be… I agree/disagree with _____ because…	The main idea of the article is…
One reason could be…	When writing an essay, you first must…
Something to always remember when _____ is…	One literary element is…
	A strategy to use when solving a word problem is…

When planning a lesson, teachers must consider the language students need for communication and understanding. In addition to key vocabulary, teachers have to determine the language function and form a lesson addresses and in what way a student needs to use it. This information can then be used to formulate appropriate stems. For example:

> *Ms. Smith has spent several days working with her English II students on drawing conclusions from reading material. They are currently reading* **To Kill a Mockingbird**, *and she has planned for students to meet in triads to practice drawing conclusions. She wants to emphasize that a strong conclusion relies on evidence so she intentionally embedded textual support and offered the following sentence stems to the groups for their conversations:*
>
> *I conclude _____ because.…*
> *My evidence is.…*

After modeling specific ways to complete the sentence stems, e.g., by using material from previous chapters and then by providing time to think about individual conclusions, Ms. Smith lets the triads begin their conversations. She monitors the group discussions and provides support as needed. As she monitors students, Ms. Smith might determine the need to provide further direct instruction in drawing conclusions, or she might realize that the stems she provided were not appropriate for some ELLs.

Why should students speak using complete sentences?

It is vital to make sure students know how to use language, and then to provide opportunities for language use. Through working with the ITELL project we found teachers were pleased with the positive effects of Step Two. During a lesson observation, one teacher modeled key academic vocabulary words in a language arts lesson using various examples. She began by defining each word, and then she provided examples. Next, she engaged students in a sorting activity. In groups, students were given a list of events and asked to place the events under the correct headings. Students were asked to use the following sentence stem to substantiate their work: *The event _____is _____ because _____.* (Castillo, 2012). She noted:

> *"I've seen tremendous growth because I am intentional about it"*
> (Teacher B, May 20, 2011).

The teacher used this activity to model and elicit key academic vocabulary in math. The teacher also noted:

> *"I have learned lots of strategies and opportunities for students to explore language without me being the one guiding every single step of the way. Now, there's lots more conversation going on in the classroom, and it's so much more meaningful."*

A pattern emerged in the ITELL teachers' awareness of how to model and elicit academic language from their students. The "academic language proficiency drives content-based curriculum and instruction" (Jimenez-Silva & Gómez, 2011).

Should students always speak using complete sentences?

No. While students should know how to use complete sentences, they should know that short phrases and fragments are sometimes appropriate. Complete sentences are important in formal, academic language, but for informal and social occasions, students can speak and respond differently. The lesson objectives determine if and when students should use complete sentences. If the objective is for students to evaluate an argument or to explain a process, then it will be necessary to use complete sentences to demonstrate understanding. If the objective is at a lower level of cognition such as, an introductory lesson on identifying planets in the solar system, then one-word responses or short phrases sufficiently demonstrate understanding. As lessons become more complex, so does the need to use more complex language to communicate understanding.

STEP 2 Summary

Academic success in the United States requires proficiency in oral English (Goldenberg & Coleman, 2010). To attain proficiency, students must go beyond basic vocabulary terms and learn to structure and speak in complete sentences with academic language. Speaking in complete sentences allows students to participate in formal ways as they acquire second language skills and internalize academic content.

STEP THREE

Randomize and rotate with peer rehearsal.

The goal in Step Three is to structure and facilitate a classroom where ALL students are engaged in the learning process. To maintain engagement, an organized structure of accountability can be established by randomizing and rotating student responses. Reeves, (2006) as cited in Schmoker, states that in 85% of all classrooms, fewer than half of all students are paying attention. Randomizing and rotating offers several beneficial outcomes. This approach provides additional time for students to process information; it gives teachers the opportunity to allow wait time after questioning; and it accommodates various levels of language proficiency. Student engagement is highly correlated with student success, and student participation inspires meaningful learning.

A higher level of student participation in classroom discussions results in higher levels of student achievement. To involve all students in class discussion, teachers must frequently use random selection so that students can respond and share their thoughts with others (Buck, 1996). Students need to find their own voices and verbally express their interpretation of course content (Morgenstern, 1992; Hauser, 1990). Skilled questioning techniques, included in the randomizing and rotating process, foster thoughtful and reflective learning and lead to higher levels of academic achievement (Gall, 1984; Dean, 1986).

Step Three has several important implications for ELLs: increased engagement, increased expectations, and increased language practice. When students do not know if or when they will be asked to respond, they are more attentive in class. Randomizing creates positive tension in the classroom and a collective understanding that everyone must be ready to respond at any time. Increased participation is highly related to increased achievement (Echevarria, Vogt, & Short, 2008). Step Three also communicates the fact that we value student input and fully expect them to participate in the lesson. In short, it builds a climate of accountability for every learner.

To involve all students in class discussion, teachers must frequently use random selection so that students can respond and share their thoughts with others. In many classrooms, when the teacher asks a question, a few students will raise their hands, and the teacher will select one of those volunteer students to answer the question. The same students continue to volunteer and are called upon repeatedly while others are neglected. To be sure that ELLs have a chance to respond, we have to randomize and rotate when calling on students. ELL students can often be the ones left behind because they are usually the quiet ones who never raise their hands…for many reasons. Sometimes they may fear making a mistake; sometimes they may have reached a frustration level; and at other times they may know the answer but have inadequate English skills for communication. Randomizing and rotating student responses can remedy this situation. When beginning to use Step Three, teachers must make sure ELLs are prepared to use the strategy.

There are three ways to prepare for random selection: wait time, sentence stems, and peer rehearsal.

- **Wait time** gives students a minute to think about the question and to formulate a response. While reflection is important to most students, ELLs need more time to process both the content and the language before each classroom interaction.
- **Sentence stems** allow students the comfort and the chance to prepare their responses. Sentence stems lower the amount of language students must produce on their own without lowering the cognitive demand of answering the question.
- **Peer rehearsal** gives students time to share responses with a partner before offering thoughts to the larger group. In addition, students can use this time to get feedback from a peer and to adjust responses as needed.

In the initial phase of randomizing and rotating, students benefit if the teacher gives subtle advance notice to those who will be randomly selected. For example, as partners are sharing their responses, the teacher can say, "In one minute, I'll be asking students with green shirts to share their thinking with the group." Or, the teacher could tap Javier on the shoulder and ask him to be ready to share after sharing with his partner.

The techniques in Step Three complement those in Steps One and Two. In all three steps, students are given the support they need to formulate responses they are confident in sharing. ***Confident students become successful students.***

"How do I implement Step Three?
How do I randomize and rotate when calling on students?"

There are many ways to randomize and rotate when calling on students. For example:

Use index cards: Record each student's name on an index card. Draw one of the index cards from the stack, and ask that student to respond to a given question.	**Organize numbered Heads Together:** Place students in groups of 4 or 5. Have each group member number off from 1-5, explaining that the number they used in the count off will be their number for the remainder of the day. Ask a question, and then randomly select one of the numbers. All students who have that number respond (Kagan, 1992).	**Hold a deck of cards:** Hand out one card to each student, then randomize by calling any of the following: red, black, spades, hearts, diamonds, clubs, face cards, certain numbers, etc.
Designate categories: Assign a category to individual students or tables of students, such as: parts of speech, days of the week, names of planets, or names of historical figures, etc.	**Place colored stickers on desks:** Place an assortment of colored stickers randomly on student desks. Ask all the reds, yellows, blues, or greens to respond to questions.	**Use individual characteristics:** Provide a starting point for randomizing and rotating, such as personal characteristics like hair color, type of shoes, or color of shirt for students to respond to questions.
		Scan the class roster or grade book: Choose students at random from the list in the class roster or grade book.

Keep in mind the following ideas as you begin to implement Step Three:

- Inclusion of all students is often an illusion without a system of randomizing.
- Student support can be implemented during randomizing when using wait time, sentence stems, peer rehearsal, and advance notice, if necessary.
- It is not necessary to randomize and rotate for every question. Once a new topic is started, students can engage in a free flow of discussion. Then student language development can continue to be supported with the techniques described in Step Three.

STEP 3 Summary

Studies suggest that random oral questioning increases student preparedness, attentiveness, and achievement (McDougal & Cordeiro, 1993). Randomizing and rotating responses guarantees that all students are included in the learning process. Using a system for selecting students to answer questions conveys these positive messages to ELLs: they are important, their learning is important, and there are high expectations for them.

STEP FOUR

Use total response signals.

Teachers must remember that, "limited English does not equate to illiteracy" (Castillo, 2012). Total response signals give students the opportunity to demonstrate their content area literacy skills without having fully developed proficiency in English. Active learning produces the greatest success (Echevarria & Graves, 2010); therefore, it is important to ensure that all ELLs, including those designated at the lower levels of English Language Proficiency, are able to participate in classroom instruction. The use of total response signals allows ELLs to participate without having to be dependent on language, and they provide an opportunity for informal assessment of each student's academic and language skills development throughout the lesson. Using active response signals has a positive effect on student achievement when compared with passive responses (Knap & Desrochers, 2009; Davis & O'Neil, 2004). Additionally, research demonstrates that the use of total response cards is highly effective with ELLs, specifically with those who are also learning disabled.

There are three critical components of a total response signal:

- **Total:** The word "total" means that ALL students must give the signal before the total response technique is considered effective. If the teacher provides only enough time for 75% of the class to signal before moving on, 25% of the class is excluded from the chance to participate. Who are the students included in the 25% left behind? Often, these are the very students for whom the signal is most important; they are the ELLs and other students who need more time and/or more support in order to participate. If teachers do not wait for 100% of the class to signal, total response signals do not have the intended positive effect.

- **Response:** In order to have a response, students must make a choice. They have to determine whether they are ready to proceed or not; they have to decide if they agree or disagree; and/or they have to think about the question. When students are required to make a choice or think through a response, they are mentally preparing an oral or written response. They do this with content-specific language, the amount of language the student uses depends upon his/her proficiency level. Even if students are not yet able to produce English, their response communicates their understanding.

- **Signal:** The signal is the way students communicate when they have made a decision, and it actively engages students. Signals should be quick and easy to demonstrate so the teacher can immediately assess the entire class.

Total response signals are especially beneficial for beginning ELLs. Students with little to no English proficiency might have great difficulty participating verbally in English conversations and discussions, but by providing them with a non-verbal signal, they are given an entry point and a way to become involved in the lesson. Total response signals are an important step toward language acquisition for these students.

Incorporating total response signals ensures that all students are included, and they allow the teacher to regularly check for student understanding. Feedback is immediate and in real time, enabling teachers to make quick adjustments to meet the needs of the students.

"How do I implement Step Four? How do I use total response signals?"

To implement Step Four, a teacher determines a total response signal students can use and then demonstrates the signal for students. The teacher also explains why signals are being used and when students should use them. Total response signals cover a wide variety of responses in the classroom. For example:

	Written Response	• Hold Up Paper • White Boards • Personal Chalk Boards • Answers on Cards
	Ready Response	• Hands Up When Ready • Hands Down When Ready • Thinker's Chin (hand off chin when ready) • Stand When You're Ready • Sit When You're Ready • Put Your Pen on Your Paper When Ready • Put Your Pen Down When You're Finished • All Eyes on Teacher • Heads Down
	Making Choices	• Open Hand/Closed Hand • Thumbs Up/Thumbs Down • Pens Up/Pens Down • Number Wheels • Green Card/Red Card • Move to the Corner/Stand Where You Agree/Stand Where You Disagree
	Ranking	• Rank with Your Fingers • Rank with Your Arm (the higher, the better) • Line Up According to Response • Knocking/Clapping/Cheering

Teachers should keep the following ideas in mind when beginning Step Four:
- Total response signals allow ELLs to demonstrate content understandings without being fully proficient in English.
- Total response signals ensure that even pre-emergent and emergent ELLs are included in the lesson.
- There is only 100% inclusion when 100% of the students have signaled.
- Support material is supplied as needed; to include everyone, be sure to provide appropriate support.

STEP 4 Summary

Using a total response signal is an active way for all students to become engaged with the lesson. Total response signals also give teachers immediate feedback that informs their instructional decisions on a minute-to-minute basis, and it helps them better meet the needs of all students. Incorporating total response signals provides ELLs with the time to think about and process new information, allowing them to participate fully in each lesson. Implementing Steps 1-4 creates a classroom system whereby all ELLs are not only included but supported. Step One focuses on explicitly teaching learning strategies to students. It is the first step toward empowering ELLs with skills to help them learn better, and helps increase student success in every learning experience. Students in classrooms implementing Steps 1-4 are consistently using, refining, and acquiring new learning strategies; they are actively engaged in the learning process; and they continually advance as skilled learners.

CHAPTER 3 Summary

The skills students attain in Step One are transferrable; they begin to learn language as well as complex content matter. Steps Two, Three, and Four continually reinforce the learning strategies from Step One in that they consistently offer students the opportunity to build language proficiency and to demonstrate content understanding.

QUESTIONS FOR REFLECTION AND DISCUSSION

1. Why is it important for teachers to systematize and facilitate an environment where all ELLs are included and supported?
2. What are teachers currently doing to make certain their classroom environment is inclusive of all learners?
3. How can steps 1-4 ensure that environment?
4. What step/s might be challenging for teachers to implement? Why?
5. What step/s might teachers begin to implement easily and quickly? How?

CHAPTER 4
Planning and Delivering Instruction in a Language-rich Interactive Classroom
Implementing Steps Five through Seven

Implementing Steps 5-7 in a language-rich interactive classroom means that teachers plan instruction aligned to the academic content and language standards of the state. These steps require students to participate in structured conversations, reading, and writing tasks.

STEP FIVE

Set Clear Content and Language Goals

Objectives aligned to state content and ELP (English Language Proficiency) standards ensure an explicit and deliberate intent to develop content concepts as well as academic language skills. Through the integration of content and language instruction, second language learners develop the ability to generate thoughtful spoken and written discourse related to content concepts. This facilitates ELL proficiency in understanding and producing texts (language) tied to specific content areas (Sherris, 2008).

According to the Center for Research on Education, Diversity, and Excellence (CREDE) report, proficiency in English involves more than the acquisition of informal and formal vocabulary of spoken English. Proficiency in English demands many other skills, including the ability to: use English conventions correctly, understand language nuances, interact with others in social and academic contexts —such as informal meetings, classroom discussions, and extended conversations, listen to or tell stories, and comprehend/explain academic content. Although these skills can be practiced without explicit instruction, the skills are most beneficial when taught through a structured process.

To begin the process, the teacher must consider content and language objectives.

58 LANGUAGE AND LITERACY FOR ENGLISH LANGUAGE LEARNERS

The implementation of content objectives requires teachers to connect lessons with state content standards (Marzano, Pickering, & Pollock, 2001). Similarly, the use of language objectives determines language skills to be developed and practiced. Teachers facilitate students' development of both content and language through accommodated outcomes and tasks (Echevarria, Vogt, & Short, 2008).

Research supports the integration of second language and academic content for effective ELL content and language development, even when students are not proficient in English (Goldenberg, 2013). In addition, the integration of content and language instruction provides a basis for language learning. Language is acquired most effectively when learned in a meaningful, significant context. The academic content of the school curriculum can provide a basis for second language learning, given the content is of interest or value to those learning.

What is a content objective and how is it measured?

Content objectives are aligned to common core and/or content area grade level state standards; they focus on developing content literacy. Content literacy can be described as the ability to think, read, write, and speak about grade-level content using academic language. Content objectives provide the context for the development of conceptual knowledge and understanding at various levels of cognition. They also provide a context for the development of academic language. They answer the question: What is the level of thinking associated with the content?

As teachers plan instruction to promote academic language and literacy, they must examine the standards and determine the following:

- What does the standard mean? What concept and/or skill does the standard address?
- What do students need to know and be able to do?
- At what level of cognition must students master the standard?
- Do the lessons from the curricular resources and meaningful tests align to the targeted level of cognition?
- Have I written a content objective that contains measurable features?

Measurable content objectives can be defined as written goals that focus on the learning standard; they include active participation of students; and they measure how well the standard is being met. Well-written content objectives contain four measurable components that answer the following questions: Who? Why? What? How? See the table on the next page.

Developing Content & Language Objectives
Features of a Measurable Objective

WHO?
(the learner)
- ☐ Students will be able to ....
- ☐ I will be able to ...
- ☐ We will ....
- ☐ I can...
- ☐ You can...
- ☐ SWD (Students Will Demonstrate)...

WHAT?
(standards)
What is being learned?
- ☐ Content standard (expectations, performance objectives, indicators, etc.)
- ☐ Language proficiency standard, language function, goal, or grammar focus

WHY?
(level of cognition/language process)
(In order to...)

Content: Why is it being learned? Is it being introduced, practiced, or mastered in this lesson?
(ie. What level of cognition are students developing?)
- ☐ Knowledge
- ☐ Comprehension
- ☐ Application
- ☐ Analysis
- ☐ Synthesis
- ☐ Evaluation

Language: What language domain is being developed/practiced? What is the function/purpose for using the domain? (indicators, etc.)
- ☐ Reading
- ☐ Writing
- ☐ Listening
- ☐ Speaking

HOW?
(Meaningful language task and specific language)
What will the learner have to do?

How does the teacher know the standard has been mastered?
- ☐ Content: Meaningful academic tasks
- ☐ Meaningful academic language tasks AND language form: Stems and/or specific language, vocabulary, and grammar

Who? Who will be learning the standard? The "who" must be determined by the teacher's written objective, and it can be written in many ways. Teachers can use the following phrases to focus attention on the learner:

- The students will be able to…
- We will…
- I can…
- By the end of the lesson I will…

Always consider the oral language proficiency and developmental level of the class when creating the "who" in the objective. The goal, however, is to be sure that the "who" question focuses on the student.

Why? Why is the objective being learned today? Teachers must identify at what level of cognitive complexity students will process the content. Will students develop knowledge of a topic or skill? Will they comprehend and apply the knowledge or skill? When writing content objectives, instruction is aligned with Bloom's Taxonomy, i.e., knowledge, comprehension, application, analysis, synthesis, evaluation.

The content of a cognitively demanding lesson can be scaffolded in subsequent lessons to support students as they master the objective at the appropriate target level of the standard. By distinguishing the "why" of a content objective, teachers can ensure a continual push through the levels of cognition within lessons.

For example:

Students will demonstrate knowledge of determining the theme of a story by defining "theme" and "topic" and then stating key points for recognizing theme vs. topic in a piece of text.

Students will demonstrate comprehension of determining the theme of a story by sorting ideas as examples of a Theme or Topic on a T-Chart.

Students will demonstrate application of determining the theme of a story by reading a short story, highlighting key ideas and inferring the "theme".

It is important to note that content objectives should not stagnate at the knowledge and comprehension levels. Research has found that of the approximately 80,000 questions teachers ask in classrooms each year, 80% are at the knowledge level (Gall, 1984; Watson & Young, 1986) and tied to low level objectives. If students are expected to master content, teachers must move them beyond the lower levels of Bloom's Taxonomy. [Note: Not all standards must be mastered and not every task must be measured.] Focused content objectives ensure that teachers plan for the correct level of cognition and measurement of appropriately aligned academic tasks.

What? What will be learned today? The answer to this question should reflect alignment with common core and state content standards that clearly outline "what" must be taught and "what" students must learn. Learning objectives or goals, found in teacher manuals, adopted curriculum, or student textbooks should not be the determining factor of "what" will be learned. Instead, the state standards should be the focus. For example:

> *The students will demonstrate analysis of the difference between plant and animal cells by…*
>
> *The students will be able to analyze the form and function of prokaryotic and eukaryotic cells and their cellular components by…*

Systematically planning the "what", aligned to a standard, provides a critical opportunity to share the purpose for learning, and it increases the probability that students will learn.

How? How will students demonstate their ability to process the content? How will the teacher measure mastery of a standard? In the content objective, the 'how' refers to the academic task that students will be expected to complete and the ways they will practice what they are to learn. More importantly, it provides a way to assess learning for the student and the teacher. For example:

> *The student will demonstrate analysis of the difference between plant and animal cells by comparing models of each cell type on a T-chart.*
>
> *The student will be able to analyze prokaryotic and eukaryotic cells and their cellular components by creating a T-chart that lists the type of cell, the components, and the functions.*

If content objectives do not provide a measure of student learning tied to standards, they do not serve a purpose. It is critical to determine whether students are accessing the information or developing the skills that match the content concepts.

What do we consider when writing a language objective?

In order to better understand the difference between content and language objectives, teachers of ELLs must understand the dual focus of their instructional efforts. The focus of language instruction for ELLs entails teaching academic English, not just teaching English. In order for ELLs to develop academic English proficiency, they must be explicitly instructed in academic English, not just exposed to or engaged in activities during English class. Teachers must understand the foundations of English Language Development based on the understanding of the three F's of language development: function, form, and fluency.

Function is the purpose for communication—why we use academic language. Some of the academic purposes for language include:

- understanding written text
- asking and answering informational questions
- comparing and contrasting information
- identifying cause and effect relationships
- conducting research
- drawing conclusions
- persuading
- summarizing
- evaluating
- justifying

Language *forms* are linguistic tools such as specific vocabulary and grammar, that are aligned with the function. Language forms are the outward manifestation of language use (Dutro & Moran, 2003). By identifying language forms and creating language structures, i.e., sentence stems/starters that align to the function, teachers of ELLs develop procedural knowledge for students to use the English language correctly.

Fluency can be described as the ease with which oral and written communication is expressed (Dutro & Moran, 2003). Oral language fluency is developed through modeling and frequent practice in a variety of contexts. Consistent and systematic practice of the language is the only way that ELLs can and will move from limited English capacity to automatic processing or fluency (Dutro & Moran, 2003).

As teachers plan instruction to promote academic language, they must examine the academic tasks students are expected to perform and determine the following:

- What language domain is the focus for the lesson?
- What is the language task? (function)
- What linguistic tools (vocabulary, grammar) are necessary in order to engage in the academic task? (form)
- How will I provide opportunities for ELLs to use the various language forms in order to develop oral or written fluency? (fluency)

Language function, form, and fluency should be evident when writing language objectives. Language objectives identify language skills ELLs need to access academic content and to develop oral and written fluency. Language objectives are aligned to grade level English language proficiency and common core/state standards and present the context and purpose for development of language production.

What are the features of a measurable language objective?

Measurable language objectives can be formed using sentence stems like:
- The students will…
- We will be able to…
- I can…
- The students will be able to…
- By the end of this lesson I will…

For teachers to write measurable language objectives, the following questions need to be answered:

Why is this language the focus of today's lesson? What language domain is the focus? What is the function/purpose for the language?
Proficiency in…
- Reading
- Writing
- Listening
- Speaking

What is being practiced or developed?
- English Language Proficiency Standards
- The student expectation for learning and using the language (function)

How will students use the language? What will be measured?
- What language forms (grammar, vocabulary, specific phrases) will be used?
- What meaningful language tasks will I plan? (to develop fluency)

When the target is language development, the answer to the question, "Why are we practicing this today?" focuses on the development of a specific language domain. The language objective will purposefully focus on developing a domain of the English language (reading, writing, listening, or speaking). By differentiating the 'why' for content and language objectives, we develop learners who can further access academic content receptively through reading and listening as well as articulate their thinking expressively by writing and speaking. This will help level the linguistic playing field for native English speakers and ELLs.

In the language objective, the 'what' ensures an explicit link to the English language proficiency standards and content concept focus that are mandated by the state and federal government. We focus on the 'what' to ensure that instruction is being provided at the appropriate grade and language proficiency level. With the language objective, we will identify how students will develop language by targeting use of specific phrases, vocabulary, and grammatical structures.

The 'how' for language objectives ensures that teachers of ELLs measure specific language forms (vocabulary, grammar, key phrases) by planning a language task that requires ELLs to use language forms to further develop fluency. During the language task, teachers monitor the ELL's use of language, and provide encouragement, modeling, or corrective feedback as necessary.

Look at the measurable features of the following set of objectives.

Content Objective: Students will demonstrate comprehension of parts of speech (verbs) by sorting actions such as physical and mental verbs.

- Who? → Students will
- Why? → demonstrate comprehension
- What? → of parts of speech (verbs)
- How? → by sorting actions

Language Objective: Students will orally name and justify what a verb is by using the sentence stems:

_____ verb is….
It is a (physical/mental) _____ verb because _____.

- Who? → Students will
- Why? → orally name
- What? → and justify what a verb is
- How? → by using the sentence stems

Content Objective: I can demonstrate knowledge of the life cycle of a frog by completing a web with verbs identifying the life cycle of the frog.

- Who? → I can
- Why? → demonstrate knowledge
- What? → of the life cycle
- How? → by completing a web with verbs identifying

Language Objective: I will write descriptive sentences using the following stems:

The first stage … The second stage … The third …. Finally

- Who? → I will
- Why? → write
- What? → descriptive sentences
- How? → using the following stems

After writing objectives, teachers clearly introduce the objectives at the beginning of a lesson, refer to the objectives throughout the lesson, and review the objectives at the end of the lesson. There are many reasons for sharing at the beginning of a lesson, the most important is to set a clear and concrete expectation for learning. Students need to be acquainted with what they are expected to learn in a lesson and how they will demonstrate what they have learned. In addition, they need time to process the "why" and "how" of the objective. Teachers can also begin the process of teaching academic vocabulary, i.e., how to identify, sort, label, and distinguish.

Introducing objectives provides teachers with a way to set the stage for ELLs to make meaningful connections to real-life.

The following strategies can be used to share objectives at the beginning of the lesson:

- Split the class into A's and B's. The A's will chorally read the objective to the B's. The B's will listen and then share the objective at their tables. The teacher will select someone from the B's to paraphrase the objectives for the group.

- Present the objective and then do a Timed-Pair-Share, asking students to predict some of the things they think they will be doing in the lesson.

- Read the objective as a shared reading piece with the entire class. Then ask students to paraphrase the objective with a partner, each taking a turn using this sentence stem: We are going to learn…..

- Ask students to do a Round Robin (taking turns), naming things they will be asked to do in the lesson.

- Read the objectives to students and ask them to listen for unfamiliar words within the objectives. Have students ask questions about the words they do not know and help them clarify the words with a visual cue or a gesture. Then, check for understanding.

Referring to the objectives throughout a lesson helps ELLs identify learned concepts and/or difficult concepts while it engages them in a self-assessment exercise. It can help students consider any cognitive strategies they have applied or need to apply to meet the lesson objectives. Referring to the objectives in the middle of the lesson helps students continue to internalize "why" the lesson is being taught and "how" they demonstrate learning during the lesson. This approach is also beneficial for teachers in that it offers the chance to identify the learning that has occurred or may not be occurring, and the opportunity to adjust the lesson accordingly.

The following strategies can be used to refer to the objectives in the middle of the lesson:

- Give students a list of academic vocabulary to "watch" and "listen" for during the lesson.
- Re-read the objective in a shared reading to refocus students.
- Ask students to determine how well they understand and meet the objective using finger symbols, i.e., *Thumbs up~ I got it! Thumbs down ~ I am completely lost! Flat hand tilted back and forth~ I understand some of it, but I'm a bit fuzzy!*

Reviewing objectives at the end of a lesson significantly helps students determine whether or not they have met the learning expectations. In this process, students internalize "who" was responsible for the learning and "what" precisely was learned. It also allows students to celebrate, to be and feel successful, and to experience ownership of their learning. They are then prepared and able to answer the dreaded question, "What did you learn today?" The answers to this question provides one last opportunity to assess and gather information, to decide what needs to be addressed next, review sections of the lesson, or to reintroduce/practice the content or language of the lesson.

The following strategies can be used to review the objectives at the end of the lesson:

- Have students rate themselves with a 1-3 –three being the highest – to answer this question: "How well did you meet the objective today?"
- Ask students how/why they can teach the concept to someone else.

- Have students demonstrate their learning and respond using this sentence stem: *I learned .... Now, I want to know more about…*
- Allow students to assess their learning with this sentence stem: *I'm not sure, I need more…*
- Ask students to write one or two sentences explaining what they learned in class today and have them give one example. This can be written in a learning log, an index card, or a post-it note.
- Have students write a Ticket-Out note to the teacher (or a letter to the parent at the end of a lesson) telling what they learned today. Their statements should indicate their understanding of the lesson content.
- Have students talk with a partner during a Round Robin. Ask students to give one example that proves they met the learning objective of the lesson.

STEP 5 Summary

Focusing on clear content and language goals begins with planning measurable content and language objectives. Aligned content objectives form opportunities for students to develop academic literacy while language objectives form ways for students to develop academic language. By integrating content and language instruction, second language learners develop thoughtful spoken and written language related to content concepts. Specific language for writing content and language objectives can be used by teachers to promote understanding of concepts and language proficiency.

STEP SIX

Have students participate in structured conversations.

Step Six focuses on creating opportunities for student conversation and discussion. Students who speak using the targeted language understand on a deeper level and create a "more durable memory trace" (Izumi, 2002). Oral English fluency is not only conversational fluency; it is the ability to use academic language well enough to be academically competitive with English-speakers (Hakuta, Butler & Witt, 2000). The use of oral proficiency is important because it promotes access to the core educational curriculum and contributes to English literacy development (Goldenberg & Coleman, 2010). Current reports agree that a correlation exists between English oral proficiency and English literacy (reading and writing) skills (CREDE, 2006; National Literacy Panel, 2006). Consequently, educators must be more directive by structuring explicit language learning opportunities that develop academic English skills. These opportunities must provide ample practice using meaningful context (Goldenberg & Coleman, 2010). Teachers who facilitate a learning environment using structured conversations provide consistent and systematic oral language practice and support for ELLs. Collaborative dialogue, in and of itself, is a source for learning (Watanabe & Swain, 2007) a new language; it creates comprehensible output and enables students to internalize the language more efficiently.

Unstructured conversation is not considred an efficient means for helping ELLs acquire academic language. According to Goldenberg & Coleman (2010), in order for ELLs to be successful, they must have "productive verbal exchanges rather than simply finishing tasks." In heterogeneous classes, it is particularly important that ELLs are adequately prepared to interact with their native English-speaking peers.

Structuring conversation requires intentional decision-making on the part of the teacher. Teachers can structure conversations by specifying the content and function (purpose) of the discussion as well as the specific language form. Such interactions can take shape as whole class discussions, small group conversations, student-to-student exchanges, or discussions of varied length, ranging from brief responses to extended conversations. Different amounts of structure can be used in these exchanges, however all structures provide practice communicating in academic English with a pre-determined focus. The critical feature to remember when structuring conversations for ELLs is to increase their English language proficiency.

Such interactions give students:

- practice acquiring new vocabulary.
- control of usage and conventions.
- comprehension of nuances in the language.
- interaction with others in different contexts, such as informal meetings, classroom discussions, and extended conversations.
- opportunities to tell or listen to stories.
- occasion to listen to or provide explanations of academic content (CREDE, 2006).

These interactions address what we know about ELLs and their needs. ELLs must ask and answer questions, summarize information, clarify ideas, offer/justify opinions, and compare/contrast viewpoints. Each of these language functions has certain phrases, language patterns, and grammatical structures associated with its form. Structured conversations provide students the opportunity to practice each of them. Teachers can frame conversations for students to practice as they ask and answer questions, state opinions (in sentences that begin with dependent clauses), or use complex sentences to compare two ideas. The fundamental goal of structured conversations is to allow students to "gain familiarity with new language forms, to hear other ways of describing academic concepts, and to hear themselves articulate an academic message" (Zweirs, 2008, p.132).

Structured conversation can also be an effective vehicle for meeting the language objective of a lesson and for allowing students to interact and practice precise language skills stated in the objective. For example, if the language objective is: *Students will ask and answer oral questions related to how the U.S. responded to Soviet aggression using: "In response to _____, the U.S...." and "What was the effect of...?"*, then an effective way to facilitate and measure this language objective is for the teacher to model the structured conversation between students. In the classroom, it might sound like the following:

Teacher: I just finished previewing everyone's notebook responses about the reasons for and the effects of the Truman Doctrine, the Marshall Plan, and NATO. Now, I want to give you a chance to practice the skill of asking and answering academic questions about the various responses of the United States to Soviet aggression. In just a moment, you will be given an assigned partner. I would like you to share the ideas you recorded in your journals.

Before we partner up, let's look at these two sentence stems:
- *In response to _____, the U.S....*
- *What was the effect of...?*

To use the first stem, "In response to _____, the U.S....," look at the section of your notes and find the reasons you recorded. Partner A will select one of those reasons and use it to complete the stem. For example, "In response to the Soviets trying to spread communism across Europe, the United States passed the Marshall Plan." Partner A should continue to explain the plan and then Partner B will ask a follow-up question to Partner A using the second stem, "What was the effect of...?" So our example sounds like this:

> **Partner A:** "In response to the Soviets trying to spread communism across Europe, the United States passed the Marshall Plan. This was a plan to give money to some countries that were hurt during WWII."
>
> **Partner B:** "What was the effect of the Marshall Plan?"
>
> **Partner A:** "It helped many European countries rebuild after the war. They were able to become strong countries again because the United States gave them money."

Teacher: After Partner A answers the follow-up question, the roles are switched and a different topic is selected from your notes. Then, Partner B uses the first stem and Partner A asks the follow-up question. Let's all practice saying these stems together, and then I'll let you work with your partners. (Everyone reads aloud: "In response to _____, the U.S..." and "What was the effect of ..."). That's, great. Find your partners and begin to discuss your notes.

Planning structured conversations for ELLs ensures teachers explicitly develop academic language which increases student comprehension of academic content. Structured conversations can also be an effective vehicle for meeting the content objective. When students have regular opportunities to talk about their learning experiences, research states that the quantity and quality of learning increases. (Schmoker, 2011; Zweirs, 2008; Echevarria, Vogt, & Short, 2008). As Schmoker (2011) explains, "Talking is not only one of the best ways to digest information; it is also a needed break and a low-threat opportunity for students to get feedback from their peers". Interaction with others is an authentic way for students to process new concepts and to express thoughts, questions, and conclusions about academic concepts.

Consider the same concept focus: Students will demonstrate analysis of the U.S. responses to Soviet aggression after World War II by recording the reasons and the effects of the Truman Doctrine, the Marshall Plan, and NATO in interactive notebooks.

> Susanna: In response to the Soviet Union trying to take over small countries like Greece, the United States established the Truman Doctrine. It was when we gave money to Greece and Turkey to help them get stronger.
>
> Felipe: What was the effect of the Truman Doctrine?
>
> Susanna: Umm, Greece and Turkey got better, I think.
>
> Felipe: Yeah, they got better. They never turned communist, right?
>
> Susanna: That's right, and, oh yeah, then they got to join NATO. I remember that was good for them because now they had other countries that would help their military fight.
>
> Felipe: So the effect was Greece and Turkey stayed free and joined NATO.

The sample interaction outlined above illustrates how structured conversations support both content literacy and language acquisition. Giving Susanna and Felipe a structured opportunity to discuss a concept helped them solidify their analysis of the U.S. response to Soviet aggression. While both students had some comprehension of the topic, their conversation gave them the opportunity to analyze the specific effect of the Truman Doctrine. Susanna's analysis resulted in a much more sophisticated understanding of the Truman Doctrine. She learned that both countries received military support through NATO, and they did not become communist countries. As they conversed, both students were able to analyze the U.S. responses on a deeper level, and they had the chance to practice asking and answering academic questions using targeted language, such as "In response to…" and "What was the effect of…" If Susanna and Felipe had not engaged in a structured conversation, these concepts would not be as clearly defined for them.

How do I implement Step Six?
How do I have students participate in structured conversation?

Implementing Step Six begins by clearly understanding and examining the content and language objectives for the lesson. The objectives dictate the nature, length, and structure of student conversations. Structured conversations should always be tightly aligned with the goals of the lesson in order to reinforce content understanding and the language focus.

Teachers should consider: What will students talk about? What language will they need in order to talk? What form will the conversation take? The answers to these questions give teachers a laser focus as they structure a conversation and ensure it is clearly tied to the objectives.

For students to then engage in an effective structured conversation, they must know what the conversation looks and sounds like. This is accomplished through explicit instruction and modeling. By modeling a sample student interaction, students see what is expected of them. This critical step is often skipped in the teaching process. With a model, ELLs can understand the expectations for both the content they should discuss as well as the specific language structures they need to use when communicating.

As teachers model the process, they must explicitly highlight new vocabulary, sentence structure, and language forms. Calling attention to these aspects reminds students of English conventions and makes them more aware of the language features they will be using. After modeling the conversation and highlighting new language features, students will be ready to engage in their own structured conversations. As students speak and interact, the teacher's job is to monitor the content and language they use and to provide feedback and support throughout the process. Though evident, the most critical feature is to have a structure. Without *structured* conversation, students interact with each other, but the interaction often fails to meet the desired outcome.

During unstructured conversations, students do not have adequate understanding of the question, what is expected of them, or which words to use when sharing. For example, conducting a Think-Pair-Share in a classroom with ELLs can result in the more proficient student doing all of the talking while the ELL nods in agreement. Structuring conversations with a clear question, an explicit learning expectation, and specific language ensures that both students actively participate in the share feature of the strategy.

A strategy teachers can use effectively across content areas and grade levels is Question/Signal/Stem/Share/Assess (QSSSA). This strategy is especially effective with ELLs as it engages the entire class. Below is an example of how QSSSA works:

Q = Question
The teacher asks a question to the class, directly linked to the lesson's objectives.

S = Signal
The teacher gives students a signal to show when they are ready to respond to the question. Asking for a signal from students builds in processing time for those that need it.

S = Stem
The teacher provides a sentence stem or starter sentence for students to use when they respond to the question. This is the teacher's opportunity to deliberately structure the language students use.

S = Share
Once all students have signaled they are ready to respond to the question using the stem, the teacher asks students to share their responses with another student. Partners talk to each other using the stem. ELLs practice listening and speaking using academic English.

A = Assess
Teachers can assess students orally or in writing.

[Handwritten notes at top: "Informal Assessment of Structured Conversations: 1) Randomly selecting students to share responses 2) Having all students write their responses"]

Teachers can informally assess the degree to which students were able to answer the question and use the language by randomly selecting students to share their responses or by having all students write their responses. Following is a sample QSSSA from a middle school math class using specific language and content objectives:

Content Objective: Student will demonstrate application of factoring equations by solving three word problems that require factoring to solve.

Language Objective: Students will speak using newly acquired mathematical vocabulary using the following stem: "One important idea to remember when factoring equations is…"

> Teacher: We've been talking about how to factor equations for several days now, and you had a chance to practice factoring equations in your homework last night. Let's take a few minutes to think about the key concepts related to factoring equations. What are some important ideas to remember when factoring equations? (QUESTION) *Four students raise their hands.* I see your hands, but I want everyone to think about this. What are some important ideas to remember when factoring equations? When you can answer my question using, "One important idea to remember when factoring equations is…" (STEM) put your pens down (SIGNAL). Let's practice saying that together.

The students and the teacher say, "One important idea to remember when factoring equations is…" Okay, put your pens down when you can finish that stem." The teacher waits for the entire class to put their pens down.

> Great! Turn to your neighbor and share (SHARE) your answer using the stem, "One important idea to remember when factoring equations is…"

The students talk to their partners using the sentence stem. The teacher walks around to listen as the ideas are shared. The teacher then shares:

> I heard several different responses to my question as I walked around the room. Let's hear from some of you. (Four students raise their hands.) You can put your hands down. I want to hear from those of you who have the color blue in your shirt. If you have any blue in your shirt, please stand. (Five students stand up.) When you share, you can use your idea or the idea that you heard from your partner, but please use the stem.

Let's all review this one more time. Let's all say this together, "One important idea to remember when factoring equations is..."
(ASSESS) All right, Gina, you're up.

Gina: One important idea to remember when factoring equations is to find the numbers that equal the constant term if you multiply them.

Teacher: Excellent! One important idea to remember when factoring equations is to find the factors of the constant term. Marco, what else?

Marco: You can always check your... Oh yeah. One important idea to remember when factoring equations is that you can always check your work by multiplying back.

Teacher: That's right, Marco. We can always check our work to see if we are correct.

The teacher continues interacting with the other randomly selected students.

More EXAMPLES OF QSSSA are included on the following table:

Question	Signal	Stem	Share	Assess
Social Studies: Why didn't settlers come to the New World immediately following Columbus' discovery?	Marker down when ready	Settlers didn't come to the New World immediately following Columbus' discovery because...	Numbered Heads together (Kagan)	Students record response on a white board
Science: How might genetic engineering affect your future?	Cross your arms when you have an idea for completing the stem	One way genetic engineering might affect my future is...	Neighbor/ Shoulder Partners	Call on the third student in every row
Math: How would this information be represented graphically?	Place pens on paper when you are ready	To create a graphic, I would...	Think/Pair/ Share	Students draw a graph in their learning logs
Language Arts: What strategies should you use when reading nonfiction text?	Thinker's chin: remove your hand from your chin when you are prepared	When reading nonfiction text, one strategy I can use is...	Conga Line	Popcorn responses: Teacher calls on first students, then that student selects next speaker, etc.

ELLs may need additional supports in order to engage in academic conversations. Explicitly teaching gestures and prompts related to the following conversation features increases both the quantity and quality of conversations for students (Zwiers & Crawford, 2009). Some examples are:

CONVERSATION FEATURE	GESTURE	PROMPTS
Elaborate and Clarify	Pull hands apart	Why do you think... Can you tell me more about...
Support ideas with examples	Index finger on pinky of other hand, palm up	Can you give me an example? Can you be more specific?
Build on or challenge another's idea	Layer hands on each other and build up	Can you add to this? Do you agree or disagree?
Apply or Connect	Hook both hands together	How can we apply this idea to our lives? What can we learn from this?
Paraphrase or summarize	Cup both hands into a ball	How can we summarize what we've talked about so far? What is the main point of our discussion?

Teachers should keep the following ideas in mind when implementing Step Six:

- Structured conversations are only effective for ELLs if they see good examples in practice.
- Structured conversations can be streamlined by addressing possible issues that might waste time before students begin their conversations, e.g. directing students who will share first; for example, the student with the darkest shirt will go first.
- Structured conversations do take time to implement in the beginning, but students continually gain academic language through practice.
- Consistent implementation of structured conversation reduces reluctance on the part of the ELL, and it sets a new classroom norm of total participation.
- Structured conversations enable all ELLs to receive comprehensible input and output.

STEP 6 Summary

Structured conversations are the primary vehicle for developing oral language fluency for students who are learning English as a second language. Oral English proficiency is important for ELLs because it promotes access to the core curriculum students are learning, and contributes to English literacy development (Goldenberg & Coleman, 2010). Current research reports agree that a correlation exists between English oral proficiency and English literacy, i.e., reading and writing skills (CREDE). Educators must be more directive in structuring explicit language learning opportunities that develop academic English. They must also provide ample opportunities for practice in meaningful contexts (Goldenberg & Coleman, 2010). Teachers who facilitate a learning environment using structured conversations provide ELLs with consistent and systematic oral language practice and support.

Structured Reading + Writing Activities

STEP SEVEN

Have students participate in structured reading and writing activities.

ELLs need multiple opportunities in every content area to read and write in response to their learning. The more opportunities they have, the more proficient they become in the English language. According to research, effective reading instruction approaches –used with native speakers in the past –are also beneficial for ELLs. The benefits, however, do not equal the same achievement for ELLs as compared to native speakers (August & Shanahan, 2006). ELLs require specific modifications and adaptations to increase literacy in reading and writing (August & Shanahan, 2010).

The components of literacy that are helpful to native speakers and ELLs include explicit phonics and phonemic awareness instruction (NLP). They also benefit from having explicit comparisons and connections made between letter/sound relationships in their native language and English. In addition, explicit writing instruction benefits ELLs, particularly when the instruction includes specific feedback on content, word usage, and syntax. Consider the following:

NATIVE SPEAKERS	ELLS
benefit from traditional components of literacy instruction	do not seem to benefit from traditional components of literacy instruction as greatly as native speakers
benefit from comprehension strategies	do not seem to benefit from comprehension strategies as much as native speakers
show a consistent, positive correlation between reading fluency and comprehension	do not show a similar correlation between reading fluency and comprehension, in limited studies (Goldenberg and Coleman, 2010)
benefit from strategies that build background prior to reading but not as much as the ELL student	benefit from strategies that build background prior to reading
benefit from explicit vocabulary instruction	benefit from explicit vocabulary instruction

ELLs do not seem to benefit as greatly as native speakers on some traditional components of literacy instruction. While there is a consistent, positive correlation between reading fluency and comprehension in native speakers, ELLs have not shown a similar correlation in the limited number of studies that have been conducted (Goldenberg & Coleman, 2010). Although both ELLs and native speakers benefit from explicit vocabulary instruction, ELLs appear to gain more in a robust approach with multiple usages, word forms, and a focus on making connections to cognates and direct instruction in word parts. Lastly, instruction in comprehension strategies for ELLs does not seem to be as helpful as it is for their native English-speaking counterparts (NLP). ELLs appear to profit much more from strategies that build background prior to reading.

Making sure that ELLs are familiar with the vocabulary and subject matter of content area reading is more crucial than it is for native speakers. August and Shanahan (2010) focus on four significant distinctions for teachers to make when developing literacy in ELLs:

- strategic use of reading
- enhanced instructional delivery routines
- adjustment for differences in knowledge
- more scaffolding

It is important for teachers to remember to accommodate reading and writing instruction for ELLs linguistically, based on their level of language proficiency. For the early stage ELL, it is helpful to provide native language and adapted text with a variety of visual and peer supports for reading. In writing, students at the beginning levels of proficiency do better when drawing or using their native language to express content concepts. Furthermore, student learning is enhanced when the teacher provides sentence stems with clear modeling.

When teaching ELLs to develop their literacy in reading and writing, teachers should avoid excessive correction of errors in content area writing. Nevertheless, teachers should still provide feedback on the language forms being used. It is important to remember that students at this level are still developing phonetic skills and phonemic awareness, some with sound systems significantly different from English. Students at higher levels of proficiency will always benefit from building background for reading, engaging in interactive tasks during reading and writing, and using complex sentence stems and scaffolded writing assignments to develop more advanced grammatical forms for writing proficiency. Samway (2006) suggests that these students should also participate in genre analysis tasks to analyze a particular type of content area writing, e.g., lab reports, word problems, essays, etc. They should identify features and sentence structures before producing any writing in the genre.

The models below show how a structured reading/writing task takes shape in three different fourth grade sheltered language arts classrooms. Most students in the class are at advanced levels of proficiency, with a few students at early stages. [Note: There are no ELL newcomers in the class.] In each example, the teacher is addressing the same topic– theme –in this language arts lesson. Notice how the third teacher integrates many of the "seven steps" into her reading and writing instruction.

Content Objective: Students will demonstrate comprehension of determining the theme in the story "Clasp" by recording summary sentences, questions and opinions at the end of paragraphs 6, 11, 17 and 23.

Language Objective: Students will orally share their ideas about the theme based on the information they've recorded using the following sentence stem: One possible theme for "Clasp" is...

Classroom #1:
Teacher: We've been talking about theme during our studies this week. I've been surprised at the low scores on your homework assignments about theme, so we are going to practice this again. The title of this passage is "Clasp." Go ahead and read it, and then pick a partner to discuss the passage. I hope you get it right this time. Start reading.

Classroom #2:
We've spent the last week talking about theme. Remember the theme of a story is the lesson we can learn from the story. It is an idea that we can take from the story and apply to our own lives.
Let's look at our visual again.

Here, you can see that we take information from the text and apply it to the real world. So today, you are going to get a chance to practice identifying the theme of a story. As you read this text, think about the theme the author is trying to present. After you finish reading, turn to a partner and discuss the theme of the story. Remember, you and your partner might come up with different themes, but that is okay. Start reading.

Classroom #3:

All right everyone, let's get settled. We've spent the last few days talking about theme, and some of you identified the theme from stories in Spanish and Arabic. Also, you shared those ideas with your partners. Remember the theme of a story is the lesson we can learn from the story. It is an idea we can take from the story and apply to our own lives. Let's look at our visual again.

Here you can see that we take information from the text and apply it to the real world. So today you are going to have a chance to practice identifying the theme of a story. Before you read on your own, let's practice identifying the theme in a short piece of text together. I'll read this example aloud while you follow along silently:

> *Audrey only liked wearing summer clothes, but it was the middle of January. Even though it was very cold outside, Audrey insisted on wearing her short-sleeved shirt and shorts to school. After several minutes of arguing, her mom finally said, "Fine, wear whatever you want." Audrey left in her hot-weather clothes and was freezing by the time she got to school. At recess, she was so cold that she couldn't play. She just stood by the wall where it wasn't so windy. Audrey was sad that she was too cold to play with her friends. She wished she had her sweater with her.*

Using our sample text about Audrey, I want you to read some examples and non-examples of theme.

Non-examples of themes	Examples of themes
Audrey should wear cold weather clothes during the winter.	It might be a good idea to listen to your parents.
Recess is no fun in the winter.	Choices have consequences.
If Audrey wore different clothes, she could be happy.	Think about the future before making a decision.
These are non-examples of theme because _____.	*These are examples of theme because _____.*

First, look at the column on the left and read the non-examples. Why aren't these statements themes? (Teachers can solicit responses from the class using the sentence stem at the bottom of the chart, making sure that students realize these statements cannot be applied outside of the story (or to the real world.) Okay, now look at the right column. Let's read these themes out loud together: (1) It might be a good idea to listen to your parents. (2) Choices have consequences. (3) Think about the future before you make a decision. Now, tell me why these are examples of themes. (Teachers can solicit responses from the class using the sentence stem at the bottom of the chart).

Now that we've completed an example together, it is your turn to identify the theme on your own. In just a minute, you are going to read this passage for the purpose of determining its theme. After you finish reading, I'll give you a chance to talk with your shoulder partner about what you think the theme is. Before you start reading, let's look at this slide to help focus your thinking while you read.

> **STOP** Stop at the end paragraphs 6, 11, 17 & 23.
>
> Think about what you just read.
>
> Write something: summary, question, comment, etc.
>
> After reading, put your **pen down** and think about…
> * What can I learn from this story?
> * What can this story teach me about life?

LANGUAGE AND LITERACY FOR ENGLISH LANGUAGE LEARNERS

First, it says to stop at the end of paragraphs 6, 11, 17, and 23. Let's take a minute for everyone to find paragraph 6. Draw a line underneath it. Take some time to do the same thing for paragraphs 11, 17, and 23 as well. These line breaks will help you remember to stop and think about what you have read. In order to demonstrate your comprehension of this text, I'd like for you to record your thinking at each of these stopping points. You may want to write a summary sentence after each paragraph. You may have a question to ask, or you might want to give your opinion. The purpose of writing something at each of these four stopping points is to take time to make sense of what you have read.

Now that you see how to break down the text into manageable pieces, it is time to read. Remember your purpose for reading is to identify a possible theme for this passage. When you have finished reading, put your pen down and think about the two questions at the bottom of each column. "What can I learn from this story?" and "What can this story teach me about life?" These questions will guide you as you work to identify a possible theme from the passage. You may begin.

(The teacher allows students to read silently. When most of the students are finished, the teacher reminds them to put their pens down and think about the two questions at the bottom of each column. The teacher then waits for all students to put their pens down to show they are ready to continue.)

Okay, it looks like everyone is ready to proceed. So my question now is, "What is the theme of "Clasp?"

Think about that question and when you can respond with this sentence stem, "One possible theme for "Clasp" is..." please fold your hands. *(Wait for all hands to fold.)* Now, I'd like you to share your thinking with your shoulder partner. Let's say the stem together, "One possible theme for "Clasp" is..." Good. Now, turn to your shoulder partner and share your theme using the stem. Once all partners have shared, let's have everyone record the stem and their responses in their journals.

The chart below allows teachers of ELL students to compare and contrast the different reading and writing techniques in each of the three classrooms shared above.

CLASSROOM DESCRIPTOR	REASONS FOR DESCRIPTOR
Classroom #1: Ineffective	Inappropriate tone No clear task/purpose No activation of prior learning No review of concepts No supports in place
Classroom #2: Effective	Friendly Tone Clear Task Activation of prior learning Visuals Student conversation Structured Writing
Classroom #3: Highly Effective	*In addition to the effective techniques used in Classroom 2, this teacher used:* Guided examples Connections to native language and culture Purpose for reading assignment Chunked text to scaffold the reading assignment Visuals for directions Structured conversation Structured writing

The guiding principle in Step Seven is for teachers to take the time to structure each reading and writing assignment. With careful preparation, reading tasks become a time for ELLs to develop and increase reading comprehension and fluency in writing.

How do I implement Step Seven? How do I have students participate in structured reading and writing activities?

Teachers can begin implementing Step Seven by thinking through the purpose, plan, and process for each reading and writing task. Answering the questions on the charts below will ensure that the task is structured for ELL success. Teachers can refer to the proficiency levels chart for descriptions of each level of proficiency. The chart offers specific indicators for what students at each language level are able to demonstrate in reading and writing.

STRUCTURING READING TASKS	STRUCTURING WRITING TASKS
Purpose Why am I having the ELL read this?	**Purpose** Why am I having the ELL write this?
Plan How will I make connections between what the ELL knows and what they will be reading? What will the student need to know to comprehend the passage successfully? What resources does the ELL need to access before they read?	**Plan** How will I make connections between what the ELL knows and what each will write? What will the student need to know to write successfully? What resources does the ELL need to access before they begin writing?
Processes What resources will the ELL use while reading? What process and/or learning strategy will the ELL use while reading? How will the ELL demonstrate comprehension of the reading passage? How will the ELL reflect on material that was read? How will the ELL reflect on the effectiveness of their reading skills?	**Processes** What resources will the ELL use while writing? What process and/or learning strategies will the ELL use while writing? How will the ELL share what was written? How will the ELL reflect on what was written? How will the ELL reflect on the effectiveness of the written material?

It is important to provide a wide variety of reading and writing tasks for all students and to give consistent opportunities for ELLs to engage in scaffolded tasks, cooperative tasks, and independent reading and writing. The following three strategies give ELLs the most balanced approach to developing both academic language and literacy:

- Scaffolded tasks provide ELLs support but lead to independence.

- Cooperative tasks give students the chance to work with others to complete a reading or writing task. Like scaffolded tasks, the goal of a cooperative task is to provide students with the support and practice needed to move to independence. Cooperative tasks are excellent opportunities for ELLs to gain additional exposures to language, and working with a peer often reduces the negative emotions associated with trying something new or difficult.

- Independent reading and writing tasks require students to work individually to build their understanding of academic concepts and to develop proficiency in academic English. It is imperative for teachers to give ELLs the opportunity to work on grade level reading and writing tasks on their own. It can be a challenge for many teachers to transition ELLs from scaffolded and cooperative tasks to independent tasks. Teachers may struggle with moving from support to independence. Nonetheless, teachers have to be able to read their audience and initiate independent reading and writing when students are ready.

The charts that follow are some examples of scaffolded, cooperative, and independent tasks for reading and writing.

Processes for Understanding and Accessing Information from Texts

READING

Scaffolding for Reading	Cooperative Reading	Independent Reading
Adapted Text Advance Organizers Anticipation Guides Building Background Graphic Organizers Margin Notes Native Language Text SQP2RS Think Alouds Taped Text Related Literature (including native language texts) Scanning	Anticipation Chat Genre Analysis/Imitation Insert Method Instructional Conversation Literature Circles Numbered Heads Together Partner Reading Prediction Café QtA (Question the Author) Reader, Writer, Speaker, Response Triads Reciprocal Teaching SQP2RS Structured Conversation	Book Reviews Comprehension Strategies Cornell Notes Double Entry Journals Field Notes Guided Notes Idea Bookmarks Outlining SSR Program Summarization Frame

Processes for Preparing and Providing Opportunities for Writing

WRITING

Scaffolding for Writing	Cooperative Writing	Independent Writing
Building Background Concept Definition Map Concept Mapping Draw and Write Free Write Graphic Organizers KWL Native Language Brainstorm Paragraph Frames Sentence Frames Sentence Sort Summarization Frames Think Aloud Quick Write	Dialogue Journals Graffiti Write Native Language Brainstorm Peer Editing Reader, Writer, Speaker, Response Triads Read, Write, Pair, Share Sentence Mark Up (with a partner) W.I.T. Questioning Written Conversation	First-Person Narratives Expository Writing: Summarization Description Sequence Cause and Effect Comparison Double Entry Journals Draw and Write Field Notes Free Write Guided Notes Journals Letters/Editorials Perspective-Based Writing R.A.F.T. Tickets Out Writing in Native Language (depending on program model)

Teachers should keep the following ideas in mind when implementing Step Seven:
- Increase student ability to read longer and more complex texts gradually.
- Increase student ability to write with greater focus and complexity gradually.
- Provide high-quality examples for students to use as references/guides in structured reading and writing activities.
- Model the thinking process and the reading/writing process consistently.
- Create teacher-adapted texts for ELLs.
- Encourage connections to each student's native language/culture and provide access to native language resources.
- Support student writing with sentence starters using key vocabulary.
- Access available resources, e.g. bilingual, ESL specialists, content teams, textbook adoption ancillary materials, and/or libraries for more ideas.

STEP 7 Summary

The same reading instruction strategies as those routinely taught to native speakers, can be beneficial to ELLs as well. However, the achievement levels between these two groups are not always equal (National Panel on Literacy for Adolescent English Language Learners, 2006). Considering this fact, specific modifications and adaptations to instruction must be applied for the ELL student. While explicit instruction in phonics and phonemic awareness is successful for both native speakers and ELLs, the ELL student needs explicit comparisons and connections between letter/sound relationships in their native language and in English. The same applies to writing instruction, especially when teaching content, word usage, and syntax. To implement these strategies, teachers can use scaffolded, cooperative, and independent reading/writing tasks.

CHAPTER 4 Summary

QUESTIONS FOR REFLECTION AND DISCUSSION

1. Why do teachers of ELLs need to plan for both content and language development?

2. What is the current expectation in your school/district regarding objectives?

3. What challenges are teachers facing when it comes to objectives?

4. How can this chapter help address those challenges?

5. Why is it important to structure student opportunities for speaking, reading, and writing?

6. What current practices are in place that support the opportunity for students to have structured conversations about lesson concepts?

7. How often and for what purposes are ELL students consistently and effectively reading and writing across content areas?

8. How can this chapter support teachers in planning purposeful reading and writing tasks?

CHAPTER 5
Systematic Implementation

The key to improving instruction for ELL students can be accomplished when school district administrators guide professional development in a comprehensive, systematic, and ongoing manner. Short-term staff development, brief follow-ups, and faculty meeting discussions are important, but the long-term changes are those that will make the difference for teachers of ELLs and their ELL students.

Progress in educational reform depends heavily on educators, individuals, and collective capacity, with a link to school-wide capacity as well. The solution lies in implementing ELL instruction systematically. A systematic approach helps the district and the school build capacity by bringing together those teachers and administrators who commit to the process of change.

In a system-wide approach, analyzing data related to ELL achievement builds a sense of urgency, and it helps teachers understand the unique needs of the ELL student population. Staff development that is too brief and unfocused lacks sufficient opportunities for reflection. Educators need time to understand the rationale behind specific educational strategies. They also need to know how those strategies relate to student data that can build high-quality changes in instruction.

In deciding the best approach, educators may continue to have debates on the types of programs that will best develop the academic skills of students whose native language is not English. No matter the program, teachers need to learn what to teach and how to teach effectively. The overriding goal is to ensure that teachers understand the issues and pedagogy relevant to the development of academic language and literacy for ELLs.

When implementing a new systematic approach, teachers must develop expertise in working with ELLs. Classrooms must be environments where both the teacher and the student understand how to challenge one another, and needs to be a place where critical thinking questions are routine. In a highly effective classroom, students practice new content when they: analyze information critically, connect to prior knowledge, and apply knowledge to the real world (Neufeld & Roper, 2003). Neufeld and Roper (2003) emphasize the following: "What students learn has to do fundamentally with how they learn it." To be able to create the type of highly interactive and cognitively demanding classrooms ELLs need, teachers must first experience their own learning in a similar environment. This can be accomplished during professional development, provided it is the right type. There is considerable evidence that the type of professional development teachers receive greatly impacts the results of their instructional practice (Castillo, 2012). In turn, this affects the way students learn in today's classroom.

The professional development process is a much needed but difficult one, since teachers may have to go through a number of changes to fully implement new instructional strategies and methods (Hawley & Valli, 1999). Hord, Stiegelbauer, Hall, & George (2006) indicate that teacher change is not an event, but rather a process through which individuals gradually become skilled in the implementation of new strategies (Kretlow & Bartholomew, 2010).

For change to occur in ELL education, professional development must be ongoing and continuous. The one-time workshop or lecture merely provides an overview for teachers. It fails to turn the theory into practice. To be certain that teachers are able to succeed, true professional development calls for the use of coaches and other teachers whose feedback becomes the instructional strategies teachers can use with their students. Forming and facilitating learning communities with teachers as part of a comprehensive approach provides supplemental opportunity for extended learning, support, and accountability as teachers improve their classroom practices.

Coaching the faculty and teachers in English language development is a necessary piece of the process when developing expertise and improvement in an instructional system inclusive of ELLs. It has become so fundamental that many districts and schools across the country are implementing strategic coaching models to build, advance, and sustain working relationships between teachers and coaches (Knight, 2007). To ensure an effective coaching model, coaching must be based on collaborative inquiry and reflection, new learning theories, and teacher practice. In addition, effective coaching needs to meet the national standards for staff development.

When coaches provide observation and feedback on the practices teachers are implementing, teachers develop a sense of accountability. Schmoker (2011) states, "You can't expect what you don't inspect." Since teacher/coach discussions give teachers the opportunity to reflect on current practices, teachers begin to internalize new practices. Most importantly, teachers determine and understand the reasons they should implement new practices.

Research shows that coaching has promising potential in closing the research-to-practice gap, and it promotes a high level of fidelity for research-based practices. In essence, coaching is on-the-job training that supports teachers when they are implementing new practices. Coaching takes professional development one-step further and allows the teacher a real-time trainer. Coaching also makes the move from abstract theories and principles–often the focus of teacher training–to authentic, everyday challenges faced by teachers in the classroom (Kretlow & Bartholomew, 2010).

Understanding the advantages of a teacher/coach relationship, a component of our research in ITELL (Institute for Teachers of English Language Learners) focused on professional development and coaching as an approach to the implementation of *Language and Literacy for ELLs*. The objective was to learn how coaching, as part of comprehensive and systematic professional development, could impact changes in self-reported teacher knowledge, skills, and classroom practices. Our research determined that coaching did impact teacher understanding and classroom application of research-based strategies specific to ELLs.

The research design included the development of an interview questionnaire consisting of open-ended and descriptive questions, focusing on classroom practice and implementation. The study took place over a two year time period. Research questions were:

- How can coaching support implementation of professional development goals over traditional development activities, as reported by the teacher, coach, and administrator?
- What is the relationship between the coach and the teacher?
- How does the coaching process relate to self-reported coach and teacher knowledge of instruction and practice in the ELL context?

According to teachers and coaches participating in the process, responses to these questions confirmed that teacher knowledge of instruction and practice specific to ELLs increased and improved. While the coaching study was qualitative in nature, principals, coaches, and teachers were happy to report that students demonstrated an increase in the development of both academic language and literacy. Consequently, this lead to higher student achievement on different types of assessments, e.g., state, district, and teacher (see table on page 8). The data for the final question in this study was the most indicative. The responses revealed the necessity to institute coaching as a component of professional development in *Language and Literacy for ELLs*. Note: It is important to mention that all educators involved in this study had ELL teaching experience, and many knew some of the requirements for students speaking English as a second language.

The outcome of the study showed that teachers and coaches gained a greater understanding of their student populations, and they were able to make a better link between theory and practice. The distinction in this study was the approach to systematic, comprehensive, and sustainable professional development and training. Follow-up support during the coaching process was determined to be equally important.

In addition, teachers indicated that both their knowledge and instructional techniques were enhanced by the coaching process. Teachers stated they were able to identify specific strategies for developing language, such as scaffolding student writing and indentifying student language levels, thereby helping them meet individual students needs.

One teacher explained that she is now able to teach language in a sound and structured way. Not only is she able to teach students to participate in the learning process, but students are learning to be personally in charge of their learning. Additionally, the teacher admittedly understands the purpose of the four language domains and has learned to incorporate them more efficiently. She summarized her new and personally meaningful experiences and acknowledged her students as learning partners. She realized that with knowledge of student language proficiency strengths and needs, language goals, and student connections, she was a more successful teacher.

In response to coaching, she shared the following,

> *"Participating in the coaching process has ensured implementation and follow-through.*
> *(Participant #3005, June 15, 2011)*

Another teacher explained how the coaching process set up a framework for instruction. Now, instruction was focused on appropriate strategies based on student language levels and literacy needs in the classroom. She explained,

> *"I now differentiate text to make it more accessible for students. I've improved content and language objectives, and I have a better understanding of both."*

She continued by saying,

> *"Also, I was more focused on the implementation of appropriate practice for ELLs with fidelity."*
> *(Participant #3006, June 16, 2011)*

Another teacher made the connection between theory and practice by saying she learned to be more intentional and specific; she knew that language development did not happen by accident. In addition, she fully understood how the coaching process affected her classroom practice. She said,

> *"What I learned in professional development for ELLs is actually happening in my classroom."*
> *(Participant #3003, June 1, 2011)*

When teachers learn to be more aware and more explicit, the ability to construct content and language objectives can be addressed more effectively.

Strategies and implementation are also important, and being accountable during the coaching process guarantees effective classroom instruction. Using sentence stems, complete sentences, and structured conversation helps students learn. One teacher said,

> *"My students are more open to using all four language domains."*
> *(Participant #3004, June 9, 2011)*

Teachers were asked to name strategies specific to the development of Language and Literacy for ELLs. The strategies they mentioned included:

- structuring conversations in academic contexts
- using total response signals
- randomizing and rotating student responses
- posting, orally sharing, and reviewing content and language objectives
- scaffolding instruction, procedures, and language
- displaying and using the "I Don't Know" poster
- grouping students based on language levels as well as on literacy needs and strengths
- teaching explicit vocabulary focused on brick and mortar words
- using formal and informal assessments
- differentiating texts

During our research, it was important to obtain the coach's perspectives on teacher progress. Impressively, their responses echoed much of what teachers had reported. Coaches shared that teachers learned to provide increased opportunities for structured and meaningful conversations effectively. In addition, the opportunities teachers were now providing for language practice were planned and aligned to state content and English Language Proficiency standards. One coach's testimony stated,

> *"The language objectives are aligned to English Language Proficiency (ELP) standards and academic language in my teachers' classrooms."*
> *(Participant #2002, June 1, 2011)*

Another coach said,

> "Teachers have increased opportunities to use language in a more structured way when planning."
> (Participant #2005, June 15, 2011)

Another said,
> "There are lots of academic conversations tied to content and academic tasks."

Another remarked,
> "There is a balance of language use between teacher and students when engaging in structured conversations."
> (Participant #2001, June 15, 2011)

Although the final research question was specific to the coach and the teacher, principals were also asked about the way instruction for ELLs and learning had been affected. Overall, principals found that teachers gained important skills and strategies that helped them instruct ELLs on a more systematic level. In short, principals observed teachers facilitating and focusing on academic language practice in the classroom. In addition, they found that students were required to do so as well.

According to one principal,

> "Frontloading the language has been used with great success; teachers have increased student discourse and given students the language they needed to be articulate."
> (Participant #1001, June 16, 2011)

Another principal stated,

> "There is more use of academic language in multiple ways; students are using structures when speaking."
> (Participant #1004, June 15, 2011)

Finally, one of the principals concluded,

> "There is conversation with complete sentences that began with sentence stems and structures…more student talk."
> (Participant #1002, June 1, 2011)

Principals were pleased that teachers realized the purpose and process of academic language activities and tasks during student participation.

To facilitate the process of systematically implementing instructional change for ELLs, the following templates offer the look and feel campuses and districts can expect. The templates follow a logical sequence based on experience with districts implementing *Language and Literacy for ELLs*. The first template discusses the beginnings of the systematic implementation process; the next focuses on identifying ELLs. The remaining templates address content and language standards, assessment of implementation of language-rich classrooms, and finally, quality lessons to ensure content and language development. Each template is divided into four columns: Reflective Questions and Actions, Expectations for Teachers, Measurable Evidence, and Research Supporting Actions and Expectations.

Reflective Questions and Actions: This column provides a focus for the other columns on the template and guides discussions about the changes during the implementation process. Based on the reflective question, an action is noted, and this provides specificity about the steps to take. Subsequently, the actions focus on what administrators and education leaders do rather than on teacher reflections and behaviors. Essentially, the questions and actions are guidelines for thinking about why changes need to take place and how those changes might be implemented. They also help teachers and administrators to begin thinking about how the changes have created success for ELLs.

Expectations for Teachers: This column outlines specific objectives for teachers to implement. These objectives help teachers structure and focus on the specific goals and actions they need to take when implementing language and literacy for ELLs. They can also help administrators find specific ways to support teachers during implementation.

Measurable Evidence: This column helps to ensure the success of reflections and expectations on the campus or district. The evidence includes such things as lists, sign-in sheets, templates, commitment forms, objectives, reflections, and lesson plans. These items help to document progress and improvement in specific areas. Measurable evidence also provides a focus for specific data when engaging in coaching conversations. In addition, the collected data can be used by other teachers, campuses, and districts that need plans for improving Language and Literacy for ELLs.

Research Supporting Actions and Expectations: This column shares some of the research that educators must consider and practice when teaching ELLs. The research includes specific considerations and implementation practices that help ELLs succeed academically. In addition, the research findings lead to improved teacher awareness and instruction.

BEGINNING THE PROCESS OF SYSTEMATIC IMPLEMENTATION
(Assessment and Data Collection)

Reflective Questions and Actions for Instructional Leaders	Expectations for Teachers	Measurable Evidence	Research Supporting Actions and Expectations
Questions • How did/do you determine what change must take place in the instruction of ELLs? • What steps have you taken to implement goals specific to the academic success of ELLs? • How have you monitored and assessed successes or continued challenges at your school when addressing the needs of ELLs? • How do you address what is not working? **Actions** • Diagnose ELL needs and how to address them. • Set goals and expectations for teachers. • Provide opportunities for teachers to develop the expertise and skills needed to work effectively with ELLs. • Set up a system to monitor progress and provide feedback to teachers.	Actively engage in the change process.	1. Signed commitment to the initiative/s addressing the needs of ELLs	Teacher commitment to the change process has a significant impact on the effectiveness of staff development (Guskey, 1986). By diagnosing the needs of ELLs to focus on their academic language development, teachers will be better able to address students' literacy goals (August & Shanahan, 2006).
	Be an active and willing participant in professional development or any learning opportunity addressing the implementation of goals set for change.	2. Attendance at Professional Development 3. Completed tasks on PD list (professional development teacher task list) 4. Teacher reflections of PD (reflective feedback)	Attending, completing tasks, and reflecting on the impact of staff development on instruction enables teachers to successfully meet ELLs' needs. Coaching of faculty and teachers in language development is necessary to develop expertise in working with ELLs (Baca & Escamilla, 2002; Echevarría, Short, & Vogt, 2008).
	Be reflective and responsive to feedback.	5. Respond to comments and questions on observation feedback forms	Working collaboratively through a process of observations, feedback, discussions, and coaching will effectively assist teachers with their progress (Echevarría, Short, & Vogt, 2008; Timperley, & Phillips, 2003).

1. Signed Commitment

I, _____, am committed to the success of my English Language Learners. Through quality professional development, implementation of English Language Development, and content-area standards, I pledge to work towards increasing academic achievement and success of English Language Learners in my classroom.

_____ date

2. Attendance at Professional Development

Date _____

NAME	GRADE LEVEL/ CONTENT AREA

3. Attendance at Professional Development

Date Completed:

_____ Signed Commitment

_____ Reflective Feedback from Sessions

_____ Observation Feedback Forms

_____ ELL Language Proficiency Levels

_____ ELL Linguistic Accommodations Chart

_____ Linguistically Accommodating Tasks-Based on Language Levels

_____ Sample Language Objective Plan

_____ Sample Content Objective Plan

_____ Sample Language and Content Objectives

_____ Sample General and Content Specific Frames

_____ Reading Planning Guide

_____ Writing Planning Guide

_____ Lesson Outline

_____ Lesson/Unit Planning for ELLs

_____ Collaboration Reflection

4. Reflective Feedback

Language and Literacy for ELLs, P.D. Reflection

Name

Date

I learned….

English Language Learners will…

I will…

I still wonder…

5. Observation Feedback

Language and Literacy for ELLs, P.D. Reflection

Name

Date

The observations and discussions helped me…

I learned…

There is something new I will try, and it is…

A question/comment I have about this process is…

IDENTIFYING YOUR ACADEMIC ELLs

Reflective Questions and Actions for Instructional Leaders	Expectations for Teachers	Measurable Evidence	Research Supporting Actions and Expectations
Questions • How would you describe the success or failure of ELLs in your district/school? • What role do you play in providing information to teachers about ELLs?	• Identify English Language Learners and their levels of language proficiency.	1. A list of ELLs language proficiency levels: L, S, R, W. (Listening, Speaking, Reading, and Writing)	Research suggests the importance of identifying different levels of language proficiency for the implementation of best practices for ELLs (Short & Fitzsimmons, 2007).
Actions • Take initiative in encouraging motivation for change by increasing awareness of ELLs specific needs in the classroom. • Identify current levels of student achievement and language proficiency. • Help teachers navigate data related to ELLs. • Facilitate thoughtful discussions about ELLs.	• Define and describe characteristics of language levels. • Describe appropriate linguistic accommodations for tasks and assessments for each level of proficiency.	2. ELL linguistic accommodations chart: descriptions of linguistic accommodations for a specific student based on level of language proficiency. 3. Description of linguistically accommodating tasks based on proficiency levels.	"Interactive instruction that provides students with opportunities to discuss content and apply vocabulary and language skills improves ELLs' academic discourse skills and facilitates improved literacy" (Francis, Lesaux, & August, 2006; Genesee, Lindholm-Leary, Saunders, & Christian, 2006; Villegas & Lucas, 2007.) Research shows that accommodating assessments to ELLs proficiency levels has a significant impact on their success. (Abedi, 2004).

BREAKING DOWN CONTENT AND LANGUAGE STANDARDS

Reflective Questions and Actions for Instructional Leaders	Expectations for Teachers	Measurable Evidence	Research Supporting Actions and Expectations
Questions • What expectations have been set for teachers about lesson objectives? • How are teachers currently using content standards to plan and guide instruction? • How are teachers currently using English language proficiency/development standards to plan and guide instruction?	• Develop understanding of content standards. • Develop understanding of language standards.	1. Sample content objectives aligned to state standards. 2. Sample language objectives aligned to state standards (ELDS/ELPS).	Research supports the importance of setting specific content and language goals to develop academic content and language skills especially for students learning English as a second language (Rea, & Mercuri, 2006; Echevarría, Short, & Vogt, 2008; Marzano, Pickering, & Pollock 2001).
Actions • Facilitate and guide teachers when identifying what students must learn, how they will learn it, and how they will meet state standards (content & ELD/P). • Provide opportunities for teachers to receive training and support on effective content and language objective features aligned to state standards. • Set expectations for writing, displaying, and communicating objectives.	• Display content and language objectives for students. • Introduce, refer to, and review objectives throughout the lesson.	3. Posted objectives 4. Reference to objectives at the beginning, middle, and end of a lesson 5. Student understanding of objectives during walk-throughs, observations, and evaluations (possible questions to ask students)	Displaying, introducing, and reviewing content and language objectives add focus and direction to the lesson and set clear expectations for students (Hill & Flynn, 2006; Echevarría, Vogt, & Short, 2008).

Sample Content and Language Objectives

Content Concept/Skill _____

CONTENT OBJECTIVE	LANGUAGE OBJECTIVE
	Listening:
	Speaking:
	Reading:
	Writing:

Posted Content and Language Objectives

Date	% Posting Content Objectives	% Posting Language Objectives	Goals/Comments

Possible Questions to Ask Students During Observations

What are the objectives for the lesson?

What are you learning?

Is there somewhere to find information about what you are learning in the classroom?

How do you know when you have met the objectives for learning?

What can you do if you don't understand?

ASSESSMENT OF IMPLEMENTATION OF A LANGUAGE-RICH CLASSROOM

Reflective Questions and Actions for Instructional Leaders	Expectations for Teachers	Measurable Evidence	Research Supporting Actions and Expectations

Questions
• How have teachers been prepared to facilitate a classroom that includes high levels of engagement for all students?
• What do you expect to see in a classroom focused on the development of language and literacy?
• What types of structured interaction should take place in classrooms with ELLs?
 	
Actions
• Identify and provide opportunities for teachers to be trained for high levels of student engagement strategies and techniques.
• Facilitate thoughtful discussions on how to involve all students in the learning process.
• Monitor and provide explicit feedback on teacher implementation.
	• Implementation of steps 1-4 of a Language-rich Interactive Classroom:
	  1. Teach students what to say when they don't know what to say.
	  2. Have students speak in complete sentences.
	  3. Randomize and rotate responses.
	  4. Use total response signals.
		1. Classroom observations of:
		  • Posted alternative strategies
		  • Posted expectation of communication in complete sentences
		  • Randomization system in place
		  • Equity in student responses
		  • Use of total response signals
			Student engagement and achievement is related to students' belief in self-efficacy to perform learning tasks (Finn, 1993; Hudley et al., 2002). Language-rich practices increase student engagement and self efficacy. Total response signals have a significant impact on the achievement of ELLs (Davis & O'Neil, 2004).

	• Explicit teaching of academic language and literacy in all content areas.
	5. Develop content and language objectives.
	6. Facilitate structured conversations.
	7. Provide structured reading and writing tasks.
		2. Classroom observations of:
		  • Posted objectives
		  • References to objectives
		  • Posted and referenced vocabulary aligned with content and language objectives.
		  • List of frames to be used in lessons
		  • Plans for structured reading
			Research suggests the importance of explicit teaching for language strategy instruction in second language contexts (Chamot, 2009; O'Mally & Chamot, 1990; Shen, 2003).

CREATE LESSONS THAT ENSURE CONTENT AND LANGUAGE DEVELOPMENT

Reflective Questions and Actions for Instructional Leaders	Expectations for Teachers	Measurable Evidence	Research Supporting Actions and Expectations
Questions • What expectations have been set regarding lesson planning? (How often? What periods or subjects? Where are they stored? What must they include? etc.) • What processes have been put in place for teachers to collaborate on lesson planning? • How are teachers expected to document specific needs of ELLs? • How have teachers been given feedback on lesson plans? • What information can you gather from a teacher's lesson plans?	• Write lesson plans (individually or collaboratively) including the components of an effective lesson.	1. Lesson plan outline	Research supports the importance of planning for the integration of content and language development (Rea & Mercuri, 2006; Echevarría, Short, & Vogt, 2008).
Actions • Determine and identify the expectations for writing lesson plans. • Identify what expectations must be set for the writing of lesson plans. • Provide explicit feedback on the components of a lesson plan.	• Establish a plan for writing effective ELL lessons/units with colleagues. • Review and offer feedback on lesson plans to colleagues.	2. Collaborative lesson/unit planning for ELLs 3. Written reflection response/feedback for colleague.	Evidence suggests that educational reforms progress depends on teachers' individual and collective capacity and its link with school-wide capacity in order to promote student learning. Capacity is a complex blend of motivation, skill, positive learning, organizational conditions and culture, and infrastructure of support learning over time (Stoll, Bolam, McMahon, Wallace, & Thomas, 2006).

Collaborative Lesson/ Unit Planning for ELLs

Date:
Sign In Names:
Grade Level/Topic:
Instructional Strategies/Techniques:
Resources:

Reflection on Collaborative Planning for ELLs

Teacher Name: _____

Date: _____   Grade/Class: _____

Collaborating with my peers on planning instruction for ELLs enabled me to …

I learned …

I will ….

We need to consider …

LESSON PLAN

Lesson:	Grade:

Standard:

ELP Standard:

Visuals & Resources:

Key Vocabulary:

HOTS (Questions):

General Frames:

Specific Frames:

Connections to Prior Knowledge/ Provide Background Information:

Content Objectives:

Meaningful Activities:

Review/Assessment:

Language Objectives:

Wrap Up:

LESSON PLAN

Lesson Analyzing and describing characteristics of geometric shapes.		Grade 4
Content Standard Concept 1: Geometric Properties: Analyze the attributes and properties of 2- and 3- dimensional shapes and develop mathematical arguments about their relationships. Identify congruent geometric shapes. **ELP Standard:** Responding to comprehension questions by comparing concepts and related facts using academic vocabulary. **Key Vocabulary:** congruent, parallel, perpendicular, angle, polygon & quadrilateral **HOTS:** What is something you learned about congruent shapes today? What is an example of a geometric shape?		**Visuals/ Resources/Supplementary Materials:** geometric shapes overhead tiles, overhead and graph paper & index cards Poem "Shapes" by Silverstein **General Frames:** They are similar/different because… Specific Frames: I created a _____ by …
Connections to Prior Knowledge/ Building Background Information: TW- read the poem SW- use geometric shapes to arrange shapes according to what they hear in the poem. SW- choose one shape and turn to a partner and share the # of sides and how many are the same. They will also share how the shapes are the same and how they are different.		
Content Objectives: 1. SWBAT demonstrate comprehension of congruent geometric shapes by showing congruent shapes using geoboards. **Language Objectives:** 2. SWBAT orally explain their shapes using key vocabulary (triangles, rectangles squares, sides, angels, etc.).	**Meaningful Activities:** 1.1 TW model on the overhead using a geoboard what one of the shapes from the poem should look like. TW describe the shape using key vocabulary. 1.2 SW in teams of two using their own geoboards replicate one of the shapes they constructed earlier in the BB activity. Students will also label the angles, sides, and type of shape (polygon, quadrilateral) on an illustration of the shape. 1.3 TW then add another shape to the geoboard explaining congruent shapes. 1.4 SW in teams work with a second team using their geoboards to model congruent shapes. 2.1 TW give each student an index card. Some students will have the illustration of a geometric shape, while others will have an index card with the description of the shape (name, angles, sides). 2.2 SW in a "Find Your Match" activity match the shapes with the appropriate description. (One student has the description, the other the illustration). 2.3 SW share their match to the group and identify another groups match that has a congruent shape.	**Review/Assessment:** 1.2 Labeled illustration with appropriate angles, sides and name of shape. 1.4 Geoboard examples. 2.1 Students identify the appropriate match and use key vocabulary to share their match with the whole group.
Wrap-up: In small groups students will complete one cloze sentence to describe one geometric shape. For example: A _____ has _____ sides. A _____ has three _____ sides… A _____ has _____ angles. A congruent shape…		

LANGUAGE AND LITERACY FOR ENGLISH LANGUAGE LEARNERS

LESSON PLAN

Lesson: Grade level, Unit and Title	**Grade:**
Standard: State content area standard at appropriate grade level. List the appropriate standard for your state and grade level.	**Visuals & Resources:** What additional resources do you need? Including those that are outside of the "regular" curriculum.
ELP Standard: Language proficiency focus appropriate to level of language	
Key Vocabulary: List key words students must know in order to understand the lesson/concept. Words they must master for on-going learning.	**General Frames:** How are you going to ensure they are using complete sentences? Provide language structures that can be used for multiple lessons. Provide them with functional language practice. For example: I agree/disagree with... I think... I understand... I will.. I can ____ because...
HOTS (Questions): Consider what higher order thinking questions will you ask? What higher order thinking tasks will students participate in?	**Specific Frames:** How will you ensure they have the language to respond to questions related to the specific content being taught? Provide language structures for students to use in one lesson. What language do they need to answer "HOTS" questions? Frames contain content specific vocabulary.
Connections to Prior Knowledge/ Provide Background Information: How are you going to connect to their own experiences and prior learning? What questions might you ask? What activity are you going to use to involve students and build connections with the new concepts? How are you going to introduce or review the key vocabulary?	
Content Objectives: What they need to have learned at the end of the lesson/PO. Should be aligned to a state standard/outcome or indicator. Must be measurable. **Language Objectives:** Consider: How will the students practice/apply key concepts, the PO and academic language using reading, writing, speaking and/or listening skills? How are you ensuring that language or ELP standards are being taught and practiced? Also has to be measurable.	**Meaningful Activities:** 1. List the activities you will do as a teacher and what students will be doing. I do, We do, and You do. 2. Number or bullet activities and be sure to align them with the appropriate content or language objectives and assessments. 3. Consider the following as you plan your meaningful activities: Are students using learner strategies? Are they being challenged? Are they using language? Are they interacting? Are they engaged? List Teachers Manual pg #'s when the activity is from the book.	**Review/Assessment:** 1. List both formal and informal assessment that will be used for each activity. 2. List Teachers Manual pg # when it is from the book or workbook. 3. Whatever students are doing should provide you information on whether student learning and understanding is occurring.
Wrap Up: Always review objectives! What activity are you going to use to close and review key concepts or vocabulary? (outcome sentences, journal, ticket out)		

Lesson Outline

Grade/Subject: Date:

Content Standard:	ELD/P Standard
Content Objective:	Language Objective:
Key Vocabulary: HOTS (Questions)	Content Specific: General Stems:
Visuals, Materials, & Texts	
TASKS Activating Prior Knowledge (Processes, Stems, and Scaffolds) Building Vocabulary and Concept Knowledge (Processes, Stems, and Scaffolds) Structured Conversation and Writing (Processes, Stems, Scaffolds)	Reviews & Checks for Understanding (Response Signals, Writing, Self-Assessment, Student Products, etc.)
Wrap Up:	

ELPS Lesson Plan Sample (Social Studies)

Grade: 8
Subject: Social Studies

Topic: Civil War
Date: 2/3/10

TEKS 8.7 A-D: Student understands how political and economic factors led to the growth of sectionalism and the Civil War.	**ELPS 3G:** Express opinions, ideas, and feelings ranging from communicating single words and short phrases to participating in extended discussions on a variety of social and grade appropriate academic topics.
Content Objective (Aligned with TEKS): Students will demonstrate knowledge of the causes of the Civil War by identifying the relationship between various causes of the Civil War on a concept map.	**Language Objective (Aligned with ELPS): (1C)** Students will express their opinions and ideas about the causes of the Civil War orally using phrases like, "in my opinion ….." "I think", "I believe that.."
Vocabulary: tariff, compromise, sectionalism, states' rights, federalism, abolitionist **HOTS:** Why were southerners/abolitionists beginning to feel frustrated? Was it just/unjust to vote on whether or not slavery should extend into the new territories?	**General stems:** I already know … From the pictures I can infer … **Specific Stems:** Southerners/Abolitionists began to feel frustrated because… It was just/unjust to vote on _____ because…

Visuals, Materials, & Texts:
Political cartoons
Two editorials, student created four-corner vocabulary

ACTIVITIES	Review & Check for Understanding: (Response Signals, Writing, Student Product, Student Self Assessment.)
Activating Prior Knowledge *(Processes, Stems, Strategies):* • Anticipation Chat • Expressing prior knowledge stems: I already know the Southerners were frustrated because… From the pictures, I can infer that Abolitionists were frustrated because…	Reviewing previous lesson orally Standing when ready Listening to student conversations
Building Vocabulary and Concept Knowledge *(Processes, Stems, Strategies):* • Scanning: Editorials & political cartoons • Read two editorials from the northern and southern perspectives • Students create concept maps in groups for the terms: tariff, compromise, sectionalism, states' rights, federalism, and abolitionist • Descriptive language stems: The main idea of my concept map is… I decided to represent _____ this way because… Some important things to know about ____ are…	Observing student work
Structured Conversation and Writing (Processes, Stems, Strategies): Conga Line with Structured Conversations from both points of view Persuasive Language Stems: "In my opinion, we should not vote on whether slavery should be allowed in the territories because…" "In my opinion, tarrifs are fair because…"	Reviewing strategy for extending conversation: W.I.T. Using Thinkers Chin Collecting student writing samples

Wrap up/Ticket out *(Choose two of the following stems):*
• Today I learned …
• I think ___ is interesting because….
• I think tomorrow we will discuss …
• I wonder …
• I want to know more about …

Language & Literacy for ELLs Walk-Through Form

☐ Teacher/Student Interaction
☐ Student/Student Interaction
☐ Independent Task

Teacher: Content Objective:

Period/Subject:

Date: Language Objective:

STEP	MEASURABLE EVIDENCE

Teach students strategies and language to use when they don't know what to do.	☐y ☐n Language learning strategies observed (instructed, clarified, or emphasized)
	    ☐ reading _____ (examples, etc.)
	    ☐ writing _____ (examples, etc.)
	    ☐ listening _____ (examples)
	    ☐ speaking _____ (IDK, scaffolded stems)
	☐y ☐n Students respond or use helping strategy and then respond
	☐y ☐n Students accomplish learning task or use helping strategy and then accomplish learning task.

Have students speak in complete sentences.	☐y ☐n Expectation of complete sentences is clearly displayed
	    ☐ Students use complete sentences - # of students _____
	    ☐ Teacher prompts students to use complete sentences

Randomize and rotate with peer rehearsal.	☐y ☐n System is established for randomizing/rotating
	    ☐ Students are given the opportunity for peer rehearsal before being called on
	    ☐ Variety of students respond- # of students_____

Use total response signals.	☐y ☐n Teacher has students use total response signals tied to content and language objectives for the lesson ☐ All students respond with response signal

Set clear content and language goals.	☐y ☐n Awareness of language proficiency of ELLs is evident
	    ☐ Documentation of language levels
	☐y ☐n Content and language objectives are clearly displayed
	    ☐ Objectives align to standards (content and ELP)
	    ☐ Objectives include academic/language task
	    ☐ Objectives are shared orally at the beginning and at the end of the lesson
	☐y ☐n Terms (related to objective) posted with **linguistic/nonlinguistic** explanation
	    ☐ Terms are explicitly explained, clarified, or emphasized
	☐y ☐n Stems (aligned to objective) are clearly displayed
	    ☐ Stems are aligned/differentiated to students' language proficiency levels
	☐y ☐n Stems are introduced/modeled/practiced

Have students participate in structured conversation.	☐y ☐n Structured opportunities allow students to engage in conversation aligned to objectives
	Teacher/student interaction is aligned to objectives observed
	    ☐ Questions asked are aligned to objectives
	    ☐ Balance of opportunity exists for student responses
	Student/student interaction observed
	    ☐ Conversation is aligned to objectives
	    ☐ Structures ensure that all students speak
	    ☐ Students use posted vocabulary/stem in appropriate context

Have students participate in structured reading and writing activities.	☐y ☐n Assigned reading task is aligned to the objective
	    Type of task _____
	☐y ☐n Assigned writing task is aligned to the objective
	    Type of task _____

Considerations for Implementation

LESSON ONE	
Actions	Persons Responsible
1.	>>
2.	>>
3.	>>
Timeline	

LESSON TWO	
Actions	Persons Responsible
1.	>>
2.	>>
3.	>>
Timeline	

LESSON THREE	
Actions	Persons Responsible
1.	>>
2.	>>
3.	>>
Timeline	

Systematic Implementation	
Actions	Persons Responsible
1.	>>
2.	>>
3.	>>
Timeline	

CHAPTER 5 Summary

Although there is no widespread evidence that coaching directly increases student achievement, according to Nuefeld and Roper (2003), there is promise. It is known that coaching does increase the instructional capacity of schools and teachers, a prerequisite for student learning.

If teachers are to be successful in meeting the needs of English Language Learners, we must first be successful in our work with teachers. We must be systematic and comprehensive in the professional development provided to teachers. Professional development should address what teachers already know and are able to do when it comes to working with ELLs, it must then provide them the opportunity and environment to learn in a way that includes effective strategies/practices tied to research based theory, critical analysis and reflection of both and application to the real-world, their classrooms, with follow up and support.

QUESTIONS FOR REFLECTION AND DISCUSSION

1. How is the focus for professional development specific to English Language Learners in your school/district currently decided on?
2. What systems and/or processes are in place to hold teachers accountable and to support implementation of what they learn as a result of their professional development?
3. Are there coaches (instructional, peer, cognitive, etc.) in your district/school? If yes, in what capacity do they work with teachers?
4. What challenges do they face in working with teachers?
5. How might the information and templates included in this chapter be helpful for a district/school?

Guide to Terms

Academic Language: Academic language is specialized vocabulary. Its structures tend to be more abstract, complex, and challenging than everyday vocabulary. Academic language is found with high frequency in classroom oral and written discourse.

Academic Task: An academic task is one that a student completes. The task could include formulating a response, solving a problem, developing a product, or completing an assignment aligned to learning objectives.

Adapted Text: Adaptations in text helps struggling students comprehend academic language. Some methods include: graphic organizers, outlines, highlighted text, taped text, margin notes, native language texts, native language glossaries, and word lists.

Affective Filter: An affective filter is the emotional barrier to language acquisition caused by a negative perception or response to one's environment.

Basic Interpersonal Communicative Skills (BICS): BICS is face-to-face conversational fluency, including mastery of pronunciation, vocabulary, and grammar. English Language Learners typically acquire conversational language used in everyday activities before they develop more complex, conceptual, academic language proficiency.

Brick Words: Brick words are the vocabulary specific to the content and concepts being taught. They include words such as: *government, mitosis, metaphor, revolt, arid, revolution, habitat, paddle, predator, adaptations, climate, grams, right-angle, polarized,* and *germinate*. Traditionally, teachers pre-teach brick words at the beginning of a content area lesson or unit. In the earlier grades, many of these words are nouns, such as *giraffe, hoof, stem,* or *leaf* –words that can be illustrated or labeled. In later grades, these words tend to be conceptual.

Chunking Input: Chunking means to break-up material into smaller units for easier comprehension. Visual and auditory information can be chunked so that students have time to discuss, attend, and create schema for organizing new information.

Cloze Sentences: Cloze sentences are fill-in-the-blank sentences that help students process academic text.

Cognitive Academic Language Proficiency (CALP): Cognitive Academic Language Proficiency (CALP) is a level of language proficiency that facilitates academic and more abstract dialogue. It is a complex, conceptual, linguistic ability that includes analysis, synthesis, and evaluation.

Common Core State Standards (CCSS): CCSS are a common set of standards for grades K-12 English language arts and mathematics, adopted by 45 states in the U.S.

Comprehension Strategies: Comprehension strategies help proficient readers understand what they read. The strategies include: prediction, self-questioning, monitoring, note-taking, determining importance, and summarizing.

Content Objectives: Content objectives are statements that identify what a student should know and be able to do in a particular lesson. They are aligned to state or common core standards; they guide teaching and learning; and they are observable and measurable.

Content-Specific Stems: These sentence stems use content-specific vocabulary. For example, instead of a general stem such as, "In my opinion...," a content-specific stem would be, "In my opinion, the Declaration of Independence is significant because..."

Content Standards: Content standards are written descriptions that outline what students should know and be able to do in a particular subject area. The expectations articulated in the content standard address the knowledge, skills, and abilities for all students in a designated subject area.

Contextualized Grammar Instruction: The purpose of contextualized grammar instruction in mini-lessons is to enable students to communicate verbally and to write more effectively.

Culture: The customs, lifestyles, traditions, behavior, attitudes, and artifacts reflect the culture of a given people.

Cultural Literacy: Cultural literacy makes it possible for students to function competently in a given society. To attain cultural literacy, students need sufficient common knowledge, i.e., educational background, experiences, basic skills, and training. The greater the comprehension level of a given society's habits, attitudes, history, etc., the higher the level of cultural literacy.

Differentiated Instruction: Differentiated instruction assumes there is a diversity of learners in every classroom and that all of those learners can be reached if a variety of methods and activities are used. To address English Language Learners, teachers change the pace, amount of work, kind of instruction, and the approach of the lesson.

Discovery Learning: Discovery learning is an inquiry-based approach to instruction in which teachers create problems/dilemmas; students construct knowledge. Ideas, hypotheses, and explanations that continue to be revised while learning takes place. (Bruner,, 1961). The discovery approach has been criticized by some (Marzano, Pickering, & Pollock, 2001; Kirschner, Sweller, & Clark, 2006) for teaching skills to novices who don't have adequate background and language to learn new content. Teachers of English Language Learners must be careful to pre-teach content area, functional language, and set lesson goals/objectives when using the discovery learning approach.

Engagement: Engagement requires meaningful student involvement within the learning environment. A fully engaged student takes part in a lesson using reading, writing, listening, and speaking skills that align to the learning objectives. Engagement is an indicator of successful classroom instruction and is a valuable outcome of school reform.

English Language Development (ELD): ELD is a dedicated block of time for students of English as a second language to receive instruction at their level of proficiency, according to state English Language Proficiency Standards. The purpose of ELD instruction is to actively engage students in learning English.

English Language Learner (ELL): An ELL is a student who is acquiring English and has a first language other than English.

English Language Proficiency Standards (ELPS): ELPS standards set clear benchmarks that reflect students' English language proficiency at various levels of proficiency and grade levels.

General Stems: General stems are incomplete sentences that scaffold the development of language structures to provide opportunities for conversation and writing in any academic context.

Instructional Conversation: During instructional conversation, students use open-ended dialogue to converse with the teacher or with other students in small groups. Instructional conversations have few "known answer" questions; therefore, they promote complex language and expression.

Instructional Scaffolding: This model of teaching helps students achieve increasing levels of independence following the pattern: teach, model, practice, and apply.

L1: L1 is a widely used abbreviation for the primary or home language of a student.

Language Learning Strategies: Language learning strategies include specific behaviors and skills that improve a student's ability to listen, speak, read, and write in English.

Language Objective: Language objectives are statements designed to promote student language development in all four language domains, i.e., reading, writing, speaking, and listening. Language objectives are aligned to ELP standards.

Language Proficiency: Language proficiency is the ability of a student to understand and speak in an acquired language.

Language Proficiency Level (LPL): LPLs define the stages or levels that identify student ability to speak, read, write, or listen in English.

Learner Strategies: Learner strategies are the mental processes and plans learners use to comprehend, learn, and retain information. There are three types of strategies: meta-cognitive, cognitive, and social affective.

Linguistic Accommodations: Linguistic accommodations provide access to curriculum and opportunities for language development for English Language Learners. The methods include: comprehensible input, differentiation based on language proficiency level, and scaffolding.

Literacy: To be literate, students have to have the ability to use and process printed and written material in a specific affective filter.

Mortar Words: Mortar words and phrases are the basic/general vocabulary required for constructing sentences. They are the words that hold our language together; they determine relationships between and among words; and they are essential to comprehension.

Native English Speaker: A native English speaker is a student whose first language is English.

Native Language: A native language is a student's primary, home, or first language (L1).

Native Language Texts: Native language texts, translations, chapter summaries, wordlists, glossaries, or related literature can be used to understand texts from content area classes. Many textbook companies include Spanish language resources with textbook adoption.

Non-English Speaking (NES): Non-English speakers are students in an English speaking environment with no acquired English proficiency.

Nonlinguistic Representations: Nonlinguistic representations include illustrations, graphic organizers, physical models, and kinesthetic activities.

Oral Scaffolding: Oral scaffolding is the process of teaching academic language explicitly, i.e., modeling academic language, providing structured opportunities to use academic language in oral expression, and writing with academic language.

Paragraph Frames: Incomplete paragraph frames provide scaffolds for language development by offering opportunities to develop academic writing and communication skills.

Question, Signal, Stem, Share, Assess (QSSSA): The QSSSA strategy helps students use new academic language during student-student interactions. The teacher asks a question and then asks students to give a signal when they are ready to share responses with another student. To respond, students must use a particular sentence stem provided by the teacher. Students are then assessed orally or in writing.

SIOP - Sheltered Instruction Observation Protocol

Reciprocal Teaching: Reciprocal teaching requires a student leader to guide the class through the following learning stages: summarizing, question generating, clarifying, and predicting. This student-student interaction involves collaboration to create meaning from texts. Palincsar and Brown (1985) and Hill and Flynn (2006) suggest adapting reciprocal teaching for English Language Learners by providing vocabulary, modeling language use, and using pictorial representation during the discussion.

Scaffolding: Scaffolding moves students, incrementally, beyond their current developmental stage or skill set and into progressively more difficult tasks.

Sentence Frames: Incomplete sentence frames provide the opportunity to scaffold language development structures that help students develop academic language.

Sentence Stems: Incomplete sentence stems provide the opportunity to develop specific language structures and to facilitate entry into conversation and writing. For example, "In my opinion…" or "One characteristic of annelids is…"

Sheltered Instruction: Sheltered Instruction is an English Language Learner approach which integrates language and content instruction. The dual goals of sheltered instruction are: (1) to provide access to mainstream, grade-level content, and (2) to promote the development of English language proficiency.

Social Language: Social language is an informal language structure that students use in relationships with peers, friends, and family.

Standards-based Assessment: Standards-based assessments measure and report a student's performance according to the ELPS and content standards.

Structured Conversation: During structured conversation, students are given sentence frames to begin a conversation, as well as specific questions and sentence starters for the purpose of elaboration. Structured conversations are explicitly planned.

Systematic Phonics Instruction: Systematic phonics instruction is used to teach sound/spelling relationships and the way to use those relationships when reading. The National Literacy Panel (2008) reported that instruction in phonemic awareness, phonics, and fluency had "clear benefits for language minority students."

Teaching Strategies: Teaching strategies are methods teachers use; these strategies allow learners to access new information.

Texas Essential Knowledge and Skills (TEKS): TEKS is the official K-12 curriculum for the state of Texas and its public schools; it details the curriculum requirements for every course. It is mandated by law.

Think-Alouds: Thinking aloud helps teachers scaffold cognitive and metacognitive thinking by verbalizing the thought process.

Total Response Signals (also called Active Response Signals): Total response signals, such as thumbs up/down, white boards, and response cards, can be used by students when responding to questions. Response signals instantly show levels of comprehension.

Visuals: Illustrations, graphic organizers, manipulatives, models, and real world objects are visuals used to make content comprehensible for English Language Learners.

Word Walls: Word walls are a collection of words posted on a classroom wall to improve literacy. Not only do they become silent teachers that remind students of words studied in class, but they provide opportunities to have language moments whenever possible. Word walls can be organized by topic, sound, or spelling. The content on word walls is changed as units of study are completed.

Bibliography

Abedi, J. (2004). The no child left behind act and English language learners: Assessment and accountability issues. *Educational Researcher, 33*(1), 4-14.

August, D. (2002). *Transitional programs for English language learners: Contextual factors and effective programming.* Baltimore, MD: Center for Research on the Education of Students Placed At Risk (CRESPAR).

August, D., Carlo, M., Dressler, C., & Snow, C. (2005). The critical role of vocabulary development for English language learners. *Learning Disabilities Research and Practice, 20*(1), 50-57. The Division for Learning Disabilities of the Council for Exceptional Children.

August, D., & Shanahan, T. (Eds.). (2006). *Developing literacy in second-language learners: Report of the national literacy panel on language minority children and youth.* Center for Applied Linguistics. Mahwah, NJ: Lawrence Erlbaum Associates.

August, D., & Shanahan, T. (Eds.). (2008). *Developing reading and writing in second-language learners: Lessons from the report of the national literacy panel on language-minority children and youth.* New York, NY: Taylor & Francis.

August, D., & Shanahan, T. (2010a). Effective English literacy instruction for English learners. In F. Ong (Ed.), *Improving education for English learners: Research-based approaches* (pp. 209-249). Sacramento, CA: Department of Education.

August, D., & Shanahan, T. (2010b). Response to a review and update on developing literacy in second-language learners: Report of the national literacy panel on language-minority children and youth. *Journal of Literacy Research, 42,* 341-348.

Baca, L., & Escamilla, K. (2002). Educating teachers about language. In C. Adger, C. Snow, & D. Christian, (Eds.), *What teachers need to know about language* (pp. 71-84). Washington, DC: Center for Applied Linguistics.

Bruner, J. S. (1961). The act of discovery. *Harvard Educational Review, 31,* 21-32.

Buck, H. J. (1996). *Maximizing student learning with the use of random oral questioning in the college classroom.* (Unpublished doctoral dissertation). Florida Institute of Technology, Melbourne, FL.

Castillo, M. (2012). *Guiding educators to Praxis: Moving teachers beyond theory to practice.* (Doctoral dissertation). ProQuest, LLC, Arizona State University.

Chamot, A. U. (2009). *The CALLA handbook: Implementing the cognitive academic language learning approach* (2nd ed.). White Plains, NY: Pearson Education/Longman.

Cummins, J. (2003). BICS and CALP: Origins and rationale for the distinction. In C. B. Paulston, & G. R. Tucker (Eds.), *Sociolinguistics: The essential readings* (pp. 322-328). Boston, MA: Blackwell.

Davis, L. L., & O'Neill, R. E. (2004). Use of response cards with a group of students with learning disabilities including those for whom English is a second language. *Journal of Applied Behavior Analysis, 37*(2), 219–222.

Dean, D. (1986). Questioning techniques for teachers: A closer look at the process. *Contemporary Education, 57*(4), 184-185.

Duffy, G. G. (2003). *Explaining reading: A resource for teaching concepts, skills, and strategies.* New York, NY: Guilford Press.

Dutro, S., & Kinsella, K. (2010). English language development: Issues and implementation at grades six through twelve. In F. Ong (Ed.), *Improving education for English learners: Research-based approaches* (pp. 151-207). Sacramento, CA: Department of Education.

Dutro, S., & Moran, C. (2003). Rethinking English language instruction: An architectural approach. In G. Garcia (Ed.), *English learners: Reaching the highest level of English literacy* (pp. 227-258). Newark, DE: International Reading Association.

Echevarria, J., & Graves, A. (2010). *Sheltered content instruction: Teaching students with diverse abilities* (4th ed.). Boston, MA: Allyn & Bacon.

Echevarria, J., Vogt, M., & Short, D. (2008). *Making content comprehensible for English learners: The SIOP model.* Boston, MA: Pearson Education, Inc.

Echevarria, J., & Short, D. (2010). Programs and practices for effective sheltered content instruction. In F. Ong (Ed.), I*mproving education for English learners: Research-based approaches* (pp. 251-321). Sacramento, CA: Department of Education.

Escamilla, K. (1999). Teaching literacy in Spanish. In J. Tinajero, & R. DeVillar (Eds.), *The power of two languages* (pp. 126-141). New York, NY: McMillan/McGraw-Hill.

Escamilla, K. (2000). Bilingual means two assessment issues, early literacy and Spanish-speaking children. In *Proceedings of A Research Symposium on High Standards in Reading for Students From Diverse Language Groups: Research, Practice, & Policy* (pp. 100-128). Washington, DC: U.S. Department of Education: Office of Bilingual Education and Minority Languages Affairs (OBEMLA).

Escamilla, K., Butvilofsky, S., Escamilla, M., Geisler, D., Hopewell, S., Ruiz, O., Soltero-González, L., Sparrow, W. (2010). *Transitions to biliteracy: Literacy squared.* (Technical report). Boulder, CO: Boulder School of Education, BUENO Center for Multicultural Education.

Finn, J. D. (1993). School engagement and students at risk. National Center for Educational Statistics, U.S. Department of Education.

Fisher, D., & Frey, N. (2007). *Scaffolding writing instruction: A gradual release model.* New York, NY: Scholastic.

Francis, D., Lesaux, N., & August, D. (2006). Language of instruction. In D. L. August, & T. Shanahan (Eds.), *Developing literacy in a second language: Report of the national literacy panel* (pp. 365-414). Mahwah, NJ: Lawrence Erlbaum Associates.

Gall, M. (1984). Synthesis of research on teachers' questioning. *Educational Leadership, 42,* 40-47.

Gándara, P., Losen, D., August, D., Uriarte, M., Gómez, M. C., & Hopkins, M. (2010). Forbidden language: A brief history of US language policy. In P. Garcia, & M. Hopkins (Eds.), *Forbidden language: English learners and restrictive language policies* (pp. 20-33). New York, NY: Teachers College Press.

Garcia, E. E., Jimenez-Silva, M., Nguyen, T., Arias, M. B., Markos, A. M., Lawton, K. C., & Diniz de Figueiredo, E. H. (2012). *Promoting educator agency: Navigating restrictive policy environments through professional development for teachers of English language learners.* Symposium Presentation at the 2012 American Educational Research Association Annual Meeting, Vancouver, BC.

Garcia, E., Lawton, K., & Diniz de Figueiredo, E. H. (2010). *The education of English language learners in Arizona: A legacy of persisting achievement gaps in a restrictive language policy climate.* Los Angeles, CA: Civil Rights Project at University of California, Los Angeles. Retrieved from http://civilrightsproject.ucla.edu/research/k-12-education/language-minority-students/the-education-of-english-language-learners-in-arizona-a-legacy-of-persisting-achievement-gaps-in-a-restrictive-language-policy-climate/garcia-az-ell-gaps-2010.pdf

Gay, G., & Howard, T. C. (2000). Multicultural teacher education for the 21st century. *The Teacher Educator, 36*(1), 1-16.

Genesee, F. (Ed.). (1999). *Program alternatives for linguistically diverse students.* Berkeley, CA: Center for Research on Education, Diversity & Excellence (CREDE), UC Berkeley.

Genesee, F., Lindholm-Leary, K., Saunders, W., & Christian, D. (2005). English language learners in US schools: An overview of research findings. *Journal of Education for Students Placed At Risk, 10*(4), 363-385.

Genesee, F., Lindholm-Leary, K., Saunders, W., & Christian, D. (2006). *Educating English language learners: A synthesis of research evidence.* New York, NY: Cambridge University Press.

Goldenberg, C. (2013). Unlocking the research on English learners: What we know - and don't yet know - about effective instruction. *American Educator,* 4-38.

Goldenberg, C., & Coleman, R. (2010). *Promoting academic achievement among English learners: A guide to the research.* Thousand Oaks, CA: Corwin.

Goldenberg, C., & Sullivan, J. (1994). *Making change happen in a language minority school: A search for coherence.* Berkeley, CA: NCRCDSLL Educational Practice Reports, Center for Research on Education, Diversity & Excellence, UC Berkeley. Retrieved from http://escholarship.org/uc/item/4sf6j3g4

Guskey, T. R. (1986). Staff development and the process of teacher change. *Educational Researcher, 15* (5), 5-12.

Hakuta, K., Butler, Y. G., & Witt, D. (2000). *How long does it take English learners to attain proficiency?* Berkeley, CA: The University of California Linguistic Minority Research Institute, Stanford University. Retrieved from http://repositories.cdlib.org/lmri/pr/hakuta/

Hauser, J. A. (1990). *Classroom discourse: Questions, quarrels, and introspections.* De Pare, WI: St. Norbert College. ERIC Reproduction. Bib ID 5527260.

Hawley, W. D., & Valli, L. (1999). The essentials of effective professional development: A new consensus. *Teaching as the Learning Profession: Handbook of Policy and Practice,* 127-150.

Hill, J., & Flynn, K. (2006). *Classroom instruction that works with English language learners.* Alexandria, VA: Association for Supervision and Curriculum Development.

Hord, S. M., Stiegelbauer, S. M., Hall, G. E., & *George, A. A. (2006). Measuring implementation in schools: Innovation configurations.* Austin, TX. Southwest Educational Development Laboratory.

Hudley, C., Daoud, A., Hershberg, R., Wright-Castro, R., & Polanco, T. (2002, April). Factors supporting school engagement and achievement among adolescents. Paper presented at Annual Meeting of the American Educational Research Association, New Orleans, LA.

Izumi, S. (2002). Output, input enhancement, and the noticing hypothesis. *Studies in Second Language Acquisition, 24*(4), 541-577.

Jean, M., & Geva, E. (2009). The development of vocabulary in English as a second language children and its role in predicting word recognition ability. *Applied Psycholinguistics, 30*(1), 153.

Jimenez-Silva, M., & Gómez, C. L. (2011). Developing language skills in science classrooms. *Science Activities: Classroom Projects and Curriculum Ideas, 48*(1), 23-28.

Kagan, S. (1990). Cooperative learning for students limited in language proficiency. In M. Brubacher, R. Payne, & K. Rickett (Eds.), *Perspectives on small group learning.* Ontario, Canada: Oakville.

Kagan, S. (1992). *Cooperative learning.* San Juan Capistrano, CA: Kagan Publishing.

Kirschner, P., Sweller, J., & Clark, R. E. (2006). Why unguided learning does not work: An analysis of the failure of discovery learning, problem-based learning, experiential learning and inquiry-based learning. *Educational Psychologist, 41*(2), 75-86.

Knapp, F. A., & Desrochers, M. N. (2009). An experimental evaluation of the instructional effectiveness of a student response system: Comparison with constructed overt responding. *International Journal of Teaching and Learning in Higher Education, 21*(1), 36-46.

Knight, J. (2007). *Instructional coaching: A partnership approach to improving instruction.* Thousand Oaks, CA: Corwin Press.

Krashen, S. (1985), *The input hypothesis: Issues and implications.* New York, NY: Longman.

Kretlow, A. G., & Bartholomew, C. G. (2010). Using coaching to improve the fidelity of evidence-based practices: A review of studies. *Teacher Education and Special Education, 33*(4), 279-299.

Lillie, K. E., Markos, A., Estrella, A., Nguyen, T., Peer, K., Perez, K., & Wiley, T. G. (2010). *Policy in practice: The implementation of structured English immersion in Arizona.* Los Angeles, CA: Civil Rights Project at University of California, Los Angeles.

Lipson, M. Y., & Wixson, K. K. (2003). *Assessment and instruction of reading and writing difficulties.* Boston, MA: Allyn & Bacon.

Marzano, R. (2004). *Building academic background knowledge for academic achievement.* Alexandria, VA: MCREL, Association for Supervision and Curriculum Development.

Marzano, R., Pickering, D. J., & Pollock, J. E. (2001). *Classroom instruction that works.* Alexandria, VA: MCREL, Association for Supervision and Curriculum Development.

McDougall, D., & Cordeiro, P. (1993). Effects of random questioning expectations on community college students' preparedness for lecture and discussion. *Community College Journal of Research and Practice,* 17, 39-49.

Meiers, M. (Ed.). (2006). *Teachers' stories: Professional standards, professional learning.* Norwood, South Australia: Australian Literacy Educators Association.

Morgenstern, L. (1992). *Action and inaction: Student and teacher roles in classroom participation.* Michigan Technological University. ERIC Document Reproduction Service No. ED 346 534.

National Center for Science Education (NCSE). *Polling American scientific literacy.* Retrieved April 24, 2013 from http://ncse.com/news/2013/04/polling-american-scientific-literacy-0014818

Neufeld, B., & Roper, D. (2003). *Coaching: A strategy for developing instructional capacity—Promises & practicalities.* Washington, DC: Aspen Institute Program on Education and the Annenberg Institute for School Reform.

Norris, J. M., & Ortega, L. (2000). Effectiveness of L2 instruction: A research synthesis and quantitative meta-analysis. *Language Learning, 50*(3), 417-528.

O'Malley, J. M., & Chamot, A. U. (1990). *Learning strategies in second language acquisition.* New York, NY: Cambridge University Press.

Ormrond, J. E. (1995). *Educational psychology: Principles and applications.* Englewood Cliffs, NJ: Merrill.

Palincsar, A. S., & Brown, A. L. (1985). Reciprocal teaching: Activities to promote read(ing) with your mind. In T. L. Harris, & E. J. Cooper (Eds.), *Reading, thinking and concept development: Strategies for the classroom.* New York, NY: The College Board.

Planty, M., Hussar, W., Snyder, T., Provasnik, S., Kena, G., KewalRumani, A., & Kemp, J. (2008). *The condition of education 2008* (NCES 2008-031). Washington, DC: National Center for Education Statistics.

Rea, D., & Mercuri, S. (2006). *Research-based strategies for English language learners: How to reach goals and meet standards, K-8.* Portsmouth, NH: Heinemann.

Reeves, J. (2006). Secondary teacher attitudes toward including English language learners in mainstream classrooms. *The Journal of Educational Research, 99*(3), 131-142.

Rolstad, K., Mahoney, K., & Glass, G. V. (2005). The big picture: A meta-analysis of program effectiveness research on English language learners. *Educational Policy, 19*(4), 572-594.

Samway, K. D. (2006). *When English language learners write: Connecting research and practice.* Portsmouth, NH: Heinemann.

Saunders, B., & Goldenberg, C. (1998). Three-year transition program for native Spanish-speaking elementary students. *Tools for Schools.* Retrieved from http://www2.ed.gov/pubs/ToolsforSchools/3yr.html

Saunders, W., & Goldenberg, C. (2010). Research to guide English language development instruction. In *Improving education for English learners: Research-based approaches* (pp. 59-64). Sacramento, CA: California Department of Education, 21-81.

Scarcella, R. (2003). *Accelerating academic English: A focus on the English learner.* Oakland, CA: Regents of the University of California.

Schmidt, R. (2010). Attention, awareness, and individual differences in language learning. In W. M. Chan, S. Chi, K. N. Cin, J. Istanto, M. Nagami, J. W. Sew, T. Suthiwan, & I. Walker, *Proceedings of CLaSIC 2010*, Singapore, December 2-4 (pp. 721-737). Singapore: National University of Singapore, Centre for Language Studies.

Schmoker, M. J. (2011). *Focus: Elevating the essentials to radically improve student learning.* Alexandria, VA: ASCD.

Seidlitz, J., & Castillo, M. (2010). *Language & literacy for ELLs: Creating systematic change for academic achievement.* San Antonio, TX: Canter Press.

Seidlitz, J., & Perryman, B. (2011). *7 steps to a language-rich interactive classroom.* San Antonio, TX: Canter Press.

Shen, H. J. (2003). The role of explicit instruction in ESL/EFL reading. Foreign Language Annals, 36(3), 424-433.

Sherris, A. (2008). *Integrated content and language instruction.* Center for Applied Linguistics. Retrieved from www.cal.org/resources/digests/integratedcontent.html

Short, D. J., & Fitzsimmons, S. (2007). *Double the work: Challenges and solutions to acquiring language and academic literacy for adolescent English language learners: A report to carnegie corporation of New York.* Washington, DC: Alliance for Excellent Education.

Smith, P. L., & Ragan, T. J. (2005). *Instructional design* (3rd ed.). Hoboken, NJ: John Wiley & Sons, Inc.

Snow, C., Griffin, P., & Burns, M. S. (Eds.). (2007). *Knowledge to support the teaching of reading: Preparing teachers for a changing world.* Hoboken, New Jersey: John Wiley & Sons.

Snow, M., & Katz, A. (2010). English language development: Foundations and implementation in kindergarten through grade five. In F. Ong (Ed.), *Improving education for English learners: Research-based approaches* (pp. 83-148). Sacramento, CA: California Department of Education.

Soltero-González, L., Escamilla, K., & Hopewell, S. (2012). Changing teachers' perceptions about the writing abilities of emerging bilingual students: Toward a holistic bilingual perspective on writing assessment. *International Journal of Bilingual Education and Bilingualism, 15*(1), 71-94.

Stoll, L., Bolam, R., McMahon, A., Wallace, M., & Thomas, S. (2006). Professional learning communities: A review of the literature. *Journal of Educational Change, 7*(4), 221-258.

Swain, M. (2005). The output hypothesis: Theory and research. *Handbook of research in second language teaching and learning, 1*, 471-483.

Texas Education Agency. (2011). *Overview of the ELL linguistic accommodations research summit.* Retrieved July, 2013 from http://txcc.sedl.org/resources/ell_materials/summit_march09/overview.html

Timperley, H. S., & Phillips, G. (2003). Changing and sustaining teachers' expectations through professional development in literacy. *Teaching and Teacher Education, 19*(6), 627-641.

Valdes, G. (2001). *Learning and not learning English: Latino students in American schools* (Multicultural Education Series). New York, NY: Teachers College Press.

Villegas, A. M., & Lucas, T. (2007). The culturally responsive teacher. *Educational Leadership, 64*(6), 28.

Watanabe, Y., & Swain, M. (2007). Effects of proficiency differences and patterns of pair interaction on second language learning: Collaborative dialogue between adult ESL learners. *Language Teaching Research, 11*(2), 121-142.

Watson, K., & Young, B. (1986). Discourse for learning in the classroom. *Language Arts, 63*(2), 126-133.

Wilkinson, A. (1970). The concept of oracy. *The English Journal, 59*(1), 71-77.

Wilkinson, A. (2007). *The importance of speaking and listening in the primary classroom: Reflecting on experience.* Retrieved from http://www.studymode.com/essays/Importance-Speaking-Listening-Primary-Classroom-107865.html

Wright, W. (2010). *Foundations for teaching English language learners: Research, theory, and practice.* Philadelphia, PA: Caslon Publishing.

Zwiers, J. (2008). *Building academic language.* San Francisco, CA: Jossey-Bass/International Reading Association.

Zwiers, J., & Crawford, M. (2009). How to start academic conversations. *Educational Leadership. 66*(7), 70-73.